Vittles and Vignettes

Books by *BARBARA SHEPHERD*

Voices in Time, *Editor*

Patchwork Skin

A Centennial Celebration of Oklahoma Stories, *Editor*

Imagination Turned Loose, *Editor*

Beads on a String – Peace, Joy, and Love, *Editor*

Vittles

and

Vignettes

A Collection of Family Recipes, Prose, and Poetry

Barbara Shepherd

Barbara Shepherd
P.O. Box 54302
Oklahoma City, OK 73154

ISBN: 978-0-9820217-4-3
1. Recipes – cooking. 2. Poetry. 3. Essays. 4. Short Stories.

Published and Printed in the United States of America
Art Affair
P.O. Box 54302
Oklahoma City, OK 73154

First Edition   November, 2015

Disclaimer: Cooking is <u>not</u> an exact science; therefore, the author and publisher accept no liability, expressed or otherwise, for any errors, accidents or disappointments for any procedures or foods made from the recipes and/or instructions included in this book.

Dedication

With love,
to my children and grandchildren.

Small cheer and great welcome
make a merry feast.

William Shakespeare

Contents

Foreword by Jennifer Eve
Introduction

———————

Foreword

I was touched and delighted to be asked to write a foreword for Barbara Shepherd. She is a warm, intelligent, thoughtful writer who has a heart for history and a love of people. Hearing she was writing a cookbook, I was more than happy to chip in with a few recipes from my family. Barbara and I discovered the art and practice of cooking 'simmers' our shared loves of family history and food.

My great grandmother, Susan Tabitha Tibbets, raised a large family on a working farm in Blue Eye, Missouri, and prepared healthy meals for her husband and eleven children. Can you imagine?? Her daughter (my grandmother) was Nova Faye Tibbets Thomas, who was an incredible woman, and cook. She was cooking good-tasting meals in healthy ways, even before it was trendy to do so. She understood the need to let the vegetables speak for themselves. She and I were very close, and I often miss her wit, wisdom, and some traditional dishes she would bring to Thanksgiving and Christmas celebrations.

Her daughter (my mother) Jo Thomas Eve, is a fabulous cook. She lives on a large property and has chickens and two vegetable and herb gardens, and even now, at 80, is always experimenting with the best ways of cooking you-name-it. As a young kid, I sat on her kitchen countertop, telling her about my day while watching her chop vegetables in preparation for the evening meal. What a legacy!

I am continuing the journey, having hosted and produced a cooking show following a 20-year career in broadcast television news. It is a heritage, and in this world of drive-through-this and microwaved-that, it is a heritage I cherish. I have two daughters, and it is such a joy to have these wonderful young ladies ask for recipes. Some of the recipes I share with them have been passed down for 4 generations.

I am so grateful Barbara is using her gift for writing to produce a cookbook that will give you some new ideas in the kitchen. With this book, she is helping make it easier for families to join together at the table to share a meal and share their lives with each other.

What a gift! Make some recipes, light a candle or two, put on some music, and talk to each other. Bon Appetit!!

Jennifer Eve   *Edmond, Oklahoma*

Introduction

Vittles & Vignettes is a collection of favorite family recipes and a sampling of my writings: short stories, magazine articles, essays, and poems, some fantasy, some factual.

Several vignettes may spotlight actual people but have been fictionalized for their privacy. Other vignettes are pure fiction but denote a time and place that's fading, like our farm families in rural America. Whether in essays, short stories or poems, I attempted to capture for you the spirit of hard-working farmers and brave pioneers who set the standards for wholesomeness in our nation. Watch any national news program and see how our country tends to look to "The Heartland" for close-knit family ties and values.

Vittles is a term used in early days for all foods. The recipes (once referred to as "receipts") presented in this book are a compilation of tried-and-true family favorites, some old, others more recent. You will find easy-to-prepare dishes for beginning cooks and some more challenging for those who have kitchen experience. A recipe is a blueprint, or pattern, to guide you when you first attempt a dish. After you've mastered a recipe, feel free to experiment by adding or deleting ingredients for a new taste that pleases you and your dinner guests. Make it your own – that's how great recipes are born.

Enjoy these stories and poems alongside a table laden with delicious foods. Preserve a piece of our heritage and pass it along to future generations so they will know of another time, one where life could be tough and unforgiving but also interspersed with pleasantries and slower-paced activities with little or no stress.

I wish for you excellent dining experiences and peace.

Barbara

Taffy Pull

Marcy looks like a model, natural blonde curls cascade down past her waist. She's pleasant, smart, vivacious, has a positive attitude and her own signature style of dress. But she has a serious side – when it comes to Christianity.

Insincere people who wear their religion on their sleeves, spouting verses and beliefs at every turn, but displaying non-Christian and sometimes immoral actions can undermine a person's faith. But, Marcy is different; she means what she says and lives a true Christian life. Wary the first time we met, I was a little concerned about her until I spent more time around her and saw that her actions matched her beliefs. We became friends and I invited her one year out to the farm where I grew up.

The smell of boiling candy permeated the back room of Grandpa's house. Coming from the hot kitchen in the ancient split-log portion of the farm house, the odor transformed the cold back room into a party atmosphere. Grandpa brought his old hay hook in from the barn, scrubbed it clean and shiny, then dried it with a striped dishtowel.

He reached high to hang the iron tool on a huge nail, attached to a clean and heavily-varnished wooden plank on the sturdy wall. When Grandma brought in steaming, molten candy on a large cookie sheet, Grandpa buttered his strong, weathered hands and gathered up the hot taffy, too blistering for anyone else to handle. Exhibiting his years of experience, he slapped the taffy onto the hay hook and pulled it like a rope, repeatedly looping the heavy mass over and stretching it from the iron tool with a rhythm that bordered on grace. After the taffy cooled somewhat and Grandpa tired, he asked Marcy if she'd like to pull.

She said, "I'd love to."

He stepped away and she buttered her hands. But, before she could start pulling the heavy rope of taffy, Marcy, of course, had to pray over it!

Grandpa's terror showed in his chiseled face and his eyes looked like they could shoot daggers. We all knew that you couldn't let the taffy cool without working it or it would harden into a giant glob. Not only would that ruin the candy, but his prized hay hook would be out of commission until we could chip away the rock-like candy with a hammer and chisel.

While Grandpa glared at his strange guest, the rest of us held our breaths, afraid our festive atmosphere had slipped into fuel for a fight.

Un-phased, Marcy concluded her prayer, verbal of course – she never did anything in silence. She stood on a wooden stool, stretched her butter-lathered hands to the still-hot candy, and belted out a couple of hymns while she pulled taffy until it was ready to slide off the hook for the last time.

Grandma came forth then to receive the "blessed candy," stretched it into a long rope, curled it back onto the cookie sheet and cut it into bite-sized pieces. We all enjoyed our taffy that year and remember it now, not as holiday candy, but as "Holy Taffy."

Taffy can be pulled between two people, being careful not to drop it, if you do not have access to a clean hay hook or similar tool. (Butter your hands generously.)

After pulling taffy, stretch it into a long rope and cut into short pieces with a very sharp knife or scissors. Wrap each piece in waxed paper, twisting the ends and store in a covered container.

Vanilla Taffy

2 cups granulated sugar
½ cup water
2½ tablespoons vinegar
1 teaspoon glycerin
1 teaspoon vanilla

Mix and boil sugar, water, vinegar and glycerin in a heavy saucepan until it reaches hard-ball stage (260°.) Stir in vinegar and pour hot mixture onto a buttered platter. When candy is just cool enough to handle, pull until very white in color.

Old-Fashioned Molasses Taffy

1 cup granulated sugar
2 cups molasses
¾ cup water
4 tablespoons butter
½ teaspoon vanilla
1/8 teaspoon baking soda

Mix sugar, molasses and water in a heavy saucepan until it reaches hard-ball stage (260°.) Cook slowly, stirring toward the end to prevent scorching. Remove pan from heat; stir in butter, vanilla and soda, then pour into a buttered cookie sheet. When candy is just cool enough to handle, pull it until it becomes light in color.

I Remember

I remember growing up on a farm, fresh vegetables from our garden, and ripe fruit from the neighbor's orchard. I remember the smell of singed hair when I held a freshly-plucked chicken over an open fire to burn away the short hairs on its body. I remember the same smell when I singed my own hair long ago. I had to beat my head with my hands and forearms to stop the fire. The small gas stove blew flames out its front when I tried to light it that day. My younger brother failed to tell me he'd tried to light it first and let the gas build up. I lived with dry, crinkled hair and without eyebrows for several weeks.

I remember the smell of burned leaves, tree stumps, and open grassland when I helped fight large fires on our farm. The weight of full water buckets and wet gunnysacks remind me how much work there is on a farm, work that has nothing to do with raising food – grains for livestock and meat for the table. I also remember cold, hog-killing days and the awful scent of fat rendering.

Memories are wonderful reminders of how things used to be and how we became the people we are today.

Today, most of us buy chickens that not only have been plucked but cut into pieces, sometimes even deboned for us. That makes cooking poultry dishes an easy feat.

Spanish Chicken Casserole

1 stick butter or margarine
1 onion, chopped
¼-½ cup chopped green chilies
1 can cream of chicken soup
1 can cream of mushroom soup
3-4 chicken breasts, cooked and torn into bite-size pieces
10-12 corn or flour tortillas, torn into bite-size pieces
1 can chicken broth, optional
½ cup cheddar cheese, grated

Preheat oven to 350°. Butter a 13"x9" glass baking pan.

Melt butter in medium-sized saucepan; add onion and chilies; cook 5 minutes; stir in soups; add chicken and simmer 5-10 minutes; remove from heat. Place a layer of tortillas in bottom of baking pan and top with a layer of chicken mixture. Continue layering until all of chicken mixture is used. (If mixture appears too dry, add chicken broth as needed.) Bake casserole for 30 minutes. Remove pan from oven; sprinkle cheese on top and bake an additional 15 minutes. Serve hot.

Posing for a Photograph

Pa, dressed in worn overalls and a comfortable shirt, exhibits extreme patience outside in the dusty street while Mama and I tie ribbons on Sara's pigtails again. We had to wait more than two hours for the old photographer to set up his big camera in the corner of the general store and get the lighting just right. Mopping sweat from his wrinkled brow and dressed like a dandy, he looks like he's outgrown his best suit of clothes. No wonder people's faces look so drawn, so angry, in their pictures. It's hard work posing for pictures for the better part of a hot afternoon.

Sara sashayed around in her new white dress, scratched at her long black stockings, and kept untying her pink satin ribbons. I stood up straight beside Mama to show that I was almost as tall as she. When we get the picture made, I can see how much taller I need to get to be her same height. My dress makes me itch even though it is made of finely-woven cotton. Mama starched our dresses more than usual yesterday so they would still look good after our trip to town in the long wagon. She wears a dress of tan satin, the same one she had worn to Grandma's funeral. With her hair piled high on top of her head and the small barrel handbag in her hand, she looks as stylish as any woman on the street. No one would know she had arrived in an old wooden wagon made to carry lumber instead of riding in a fancy carriage, maybe one with fringe on top.

Pa refused to have his picture made and decided to stay outside. Someone needed to keep the mules content anyway. But, they weren't as confused today as usual, so the ride into town went as smooth as fresh-spun linen.

At home, Mama usually drives the lumber wagon while Pa loads slender tree trunks on it from the woods. Although all mules seem to know that "gee" means right and "haw" means left, our mules, Hank and Joe, really have to concentrate on commands. Mama gets them riled up when she says gee but pulls on the reins to get them to turn left. Haw is just as bad. She knows what gee and haw mean, but Mama always intends the opposite. We're used to it. When she says to pass the gravy to the left, she hands the hot bowl to me, sitting on her right. Pa tried to correct her, but after fifteen years, he has given up. She's driven Hank and Joe for half that time, but they still get mixed up with Mama playing mule-skinner.

Now, the photographer says, "I finally have it. Stand real still."

We stand up straight and he says to Mama, "Put your right arm behind Sara and hold your handbag in your left."

Mama says, "Yes, sir." Then, she promptly puts her left arm behind Sara and brings her right one forward with the barrel handbag hanging from the long fingers of her right hand.

The photographer's face turns deep red like a ripe beet but I whisper for him to take the picture *now*. He pulls his timepiece from his watch pocket, looks at the late hour, then ducks his head under the camera's canopy and clicks. The small explosion startles us, but he promises us it will be a great picture. I've never been so relieved to walk out into the July sunshine to let the mules take us home.

Any month is a perfect time to make ice cream but, because of Independence Day celebrations, July tops the list. I remember making ice cream every July 4ᵗʰ. Be-fore we had electricity for kitchen appliances, we had to keep our foods chilled in a real "ice box." We had to drive five miles into town to buy ice from an icehouse and try to keep the big block of ice from melting on our way back home.

Homemade Ice Cream

4 large eggs (or 6 medium)
2 cups granulated sugar
1 package ice cream mix (also referred to as Junket)
1 tablespoon vanilla
2 (12-ounce) cans evaporated milk
1 teaspoon other flavoring, optional
    (lemon, pineapple, rum, coconut, or orange extract)
Whole milk, as needed

Mix eggs, sugar, ice cream mix, vanilla and evaporated milk in large bowl with pouring spout. Add 1 teaspoon of one of the other flavorings, if desired. Pour mixture into 1-gallon container of ice cream freezer and fill to within 3-4 inches from top of container with whole milk.

Insert paddle, cover and process with lots of ice and rock salt in outside section of ice cream freezer. Serve immediately.

Women's Words

Anxious to hear stories, Brenna listens at my knee,
both of us enraptured with a fragile book.
Canned seven quarts tomatoes, penciled in the tattered
diary by Grandma Gertie, describes one August day.
Eager to make iced tea, Grandma sent her
firstborn son outside after a storm to pick up hailstones.
Genealogy in a few words gives us an accurate
history of her daily life,
images of an ancestor documented nowhere else.
Journaling by Grandpa vanished long ago,
kindred spirits, he and Grandma. She saved
love letters from him, pages now yellowed.
Mama's fine hand records Grandma's death on the last page,
neat, never hurried, precise, like calligraphy.
Over seventy years ago, Mama received
perfect penmanship awards in school,
quill pens dipped in blue ink bottles for her tools.
Robust, yet petite, Great-Grandma Cooper had no time to write, her
stories verbal, fairy tales voiced over the din and
trials of raising seventeen kids. My granddaughter and I
uncover a treasure of memories in Grandma Gertie's diary and
verify our matriarchal line. An old
will flutters out, signed by an
X, because Great-Great-Grandma Hopkins couldn't write.
Years of words surround us while Brenna and I sit beside
zinnias and scribble in our own diaries.

Grandma Scott's Cole Slaw

1 large head cabbage, shredded
1 large onion, chopped
1 large green bell pepper, chopped
1 cup sugar
¾ cup salad oil
1 cup white or apple cider vinegar
1 teaspoon mustard seed
1 teaspoon celery seed
1 tablespoon salt

In large bowl, spread layers of cabbage, onion and pepper until all is used; sprinkle sugar over vegetables. Combine oil, vinegar, seeds, and salt in small saucepan; bring to a boil; remove from heat and pour over cabbage mixture. Cover and chill in refrigerator.

Just before serving, stir vegetables to re-mix oil and vinegar.

Forever Young

Debra H. celebrates her 13th birthday this month, but she's already a grandmother. A four-year-old boy, nicknamed Jaybird, knows her as "Granny."

If she'd been born a day earlier or a day later, this would be Debra's 52nd birthday. However, she was born in a leap year (on a February 29th) and gets cheated out of her own special day 75% of the time. But, that's not how she sees it.

According to Debra, "It's different. It's really kind of fun." When she shows her driver's license to cashiers for identification, she hears, "February 29th? That's special. I never knew *anyone* born on that day."

Most of us look at the 29th of February as an extra day to work or play, but it means Debra need not borrow someone else's birthdate to enjoy cake, ice cream, balloons and presents. She chooses February 28th for each of the three years in between leap years.

Unlike a teen who celebrates her official 13th birthday year, the young grandma needs no calendar to remind her that 13 actual birthdays, for her and other leap year babies, count up pretty fast.

An avid reader, creative cook, and gifted home decorator, Debra gets to blow out birthday candles on her very own day this year for the thirteenth time. At this rate, Jaybird's "Granny" will stay young forever.

Debra's mother, Floria, shared her recipe for a delicious carrot salad. It makes a big bowlful but keeps well in the refrigerator for a few days. (A great dish to take to potlucks.)

Carrot Relish

2 pounds carrots, peeled and sliced in 1½-inch diagonal pieces
1 or 2 red onions, peeled and chopped
1 or 2 green bell peppers, chopped
1 cup sugar
¾ cup red wine vinegar
½ cup vegetable oil
1 teaspoon Worcestershire sauce

Cook carrots in a pan of boiling water or steamer until just tender. Drain carrots well and place in a large mixing bowl; add onions and peppers. Heat sugar, vinegar, oil, and Worcestershire sauce in a small saucepan until sugar is dissolved; pour over carrot mixture. Cover and chill several hours or overnight.

Just before serving, stir vegetables to re-mix oil and vinegar.

Need More Time?

Leap Year comes every 4th year, always on an even year, and I never see it as the extra day that it provides. I should treat it as a holiday – a gift of time – 24 hours that I can use any way that I choose. Instead, I usually work, at the office, or in my home office, and that special time disappears just as fast as regular days off.

This year will be different. I have a month to plan ahead, to look before I leap – into doing laundry or paying bills or some other non-rewarding activity.

I may leap into my boss's office and put in for a vacation day for February 29th. Not to go anywhere, although I could, but just to have a day specifically set aside for myself.

"Leapin' lizards," he'll say, but he might sign my request. If he does, I can bound out of his office and leap frog over the copier or leap about the office like a ballet dancer. Freedom, mixed with glee, will race through me.

But, then comes the waiting, anticipation for the day that's like a present. Will I use it wisely?

Will I look back later and be able to say what I did with the extra time? Maybe not. Probably not. I won't know how to act with time on my hands. That's a foreign concept to me. But, even if I do nothing but sleep, it's my day. There aren't many of those – days where I can put myself first. It's way past time I did that.

I'm knocking hard on 60's door, so I have no idea how much time I have left on earth. I've probably wasted February 29th of the first 14 leap years I've seen. I certainly can't remember doing anything special. But now, it's time.

Call it a leap of faith. Faith that I'll see many more leap years and that I'll set aside that special February day in each one of them to enjoy something wonderful.

How about you? What will you do with your extra 24 hours?

When you have a sudden gift of time, put something in the slow cooker so you'll have a good meal at the end of the day but not be tied to the stove; then, do something you said you've always wanted to do for the rest of "your special day." Or, be adventurous; try something new.

Pulled Pork Tenderloin

1 package pork tenderloin (unseasoned)
1 bottle Pick-a-Peppa® Sauce
1 jar apricot preserves

Put these three ingredients in a slow cooker, curling the tenderloin to fit inside. Cook on low for 6 hours, or on high for 4.
Using two forks, shred the meat.

Serving suggestions:
1. Wonderful on slider rolls, or just by itself.
2. Great with a salad and wild rice.

Note: I love this recipe and make it often, using half the bottle of sauce each time. Using the recipe as is with the full bottle, I've cooked pork loin too, cutting the meat to fit the slow cooker. The sauce can be found on the store aisle beside condiments like steak sauce and hot sauce. Jennifer Eve and her daughters shared this recipe with me when I interviewed them for a magazine article ten years ago.

Jennifer Eve's New Syndicated Series
Focuses on Family

No stranger to a microphone, television personality Jennifer Eve rarely speaks into a mic at fast-food restaurants to order a quick dinner for her family. She contends that when we eat that kind of non-nutritious and calorie-laden foods, our families pay the price. "Childhood obesity is an epidemic," Eve says, and she is determined to do something about it!

Cooking meals is not always given the priority it deserves these days and some people are intimidated when they step into a kitchen. "They simply do not know how to cook. The art of cooking is becoming a lost art," Eve says.

She quotes George Bush, "Families can help secure a healthy tomorrow for their children by providing guidance, staying involved, and serving as role models." Eve feels fortunate that she had a good role model when her stay-at-home mother cooked nutritious meals. Now comfortable in her own kitchen, Eve says she learned to cook by watching her mother. But not all mothers can be at home today or find the time to cook.

Jennifer Eve's mission is to bring families and friends back together at the dinner table to talk and laugh, to share memories and make new ones. But how can a busy parent prepare healthy meals for all those hungry people gathered around the dinner table?

Enter *Together at the Table*, a new syndicated series for TV, produced and hosted by former award-winning news anchor Jennifer Eve. Its focus is to encourage families to eat at home more often and to teach viewers how to cook quick but healthy meals. Joining Eve in this project are Lanell Olson, a registered dietitian and nutrition instructor, and Jerry Hart, an Emmy award-winning producer. Other impressive honors and awards for this team are listed on their newly-launched website: www.togetheratthetable.com

Each segment of News 9 *Together at the Table* airs on Oklahoma City's KWTV during its Wednesday Noon News and repeats on the Sunday Morning News.

Viewing herself as a "full-time career person and a full-time stay-at-home mom," Eve has found the best of both worlds.

As an Edmond resident with her husband Mark Fish, two delightful children, about thirty fish, guinea pigs Sweetie and

Angel, the cat Victoria, and Fabulous Frasier the Sheltie, Eve is busy meeting deadlines. She owns Jennifer Eve Media, Inc., teaches a Polishing Your Performance journalism class at UCO and volunteers for her children's school functions. How does she accomplish all of this?

Planning is key for Eve, but it's her two-fold passion that keeps her on track. She wants to take the fear out of the kitchen so others can cook healthy food for their families and continue the tradition of sitting down at the dinner table.

Families are so disconnected," Eve says, noting several studies that demonstrate the positive effects of families dining together. The old-fashioned activity of eating family meals has been shown to increase communication and social skills and to improve nutritional dietary intake. Multiple research studies also attest to reducing the risks of adolescent smoking, drug and alcohol abuse, depression and suicide – all influenced by the frequency of family meals.

Sitting on the kitchen counter as a little girl while her mother chopped onions and celery is one of Eve's fondest memories. That time spent talking with her mother and years of sit-down family dinners made an impact on Eve who doesn't want to see the dinnertime ritual disappear. She wants her children to continue this tradition, to pass it on to the next generation, and the next, and she hopes others will do the same.

Women have worked outside the home for decades now and some customs have been put on the back burner – where the pan of roast used to simmer. With a new awareness of how easy it is to cook, a collection of recipes from *Together at the Table* addresses the problem of finding the time to cook. Eve's desire to "pass down the art of cooking" could revive (or start) the traditional evening meal for many households.

Tradition is evident in Eve's home where her family dines together six or seven nights a week – every week. Daughters Elizabeth, eleven, and Olivia, nine, help set the table, turn on soft music, light candles, and sometimes assist in the kitchen – the same kitchen seen on TV.

The girls will appear in several segments of *Together at the Table*. Besides learning how to cook, they also know how to eat healthy foods. Elizabeth says, "There's always something mixed in with the vegetables; they're not just plain." Olivia says, "We have salad every night." The girls say it's true that their mother stops by for fast food – about three or four times a year!

How does one get children to eat vegetables like that? If parents serve a variety of vegetables on a regular basis, children are more likely to taste-test vegetables new to them and may find they actually like them. Broiling or sautéing vegetables, instead of boiling or steaming, can change a food's texture and may make it more palatable for a novice epicurean. An easy way to introduce new vegetables is to add them to a soup or stew. Or, prepare a recipe in a slow cooker that makes a whole meal: meat, vegetables, and sauce.

Jennifer Eve's favorite meal is "anything Mediterranean" and her favorite dish is Mediterranean Chicken. As for preparation, she loves to make soups.

Improving nutritional health could be reason enough for eating family meals together. But when the simple act of dining together at the table could produce so many other benefits, how can one not throw something in the Crock-Pot® in the morning before going to work and schedule the time to sit down with family members in the evening?

Article by Barbara Shepherd in the November 2005 Issue of Edmond Outlook

Mediterranean Chicken a la Jennifer

1 whole chicken, cut up (or 4 chicken breasts or 6 thighs)
2 tablespoons cooking oil
1 (14.5 ounce) can diced tomatoes, undrained
½ envelope onion soup mix
1 (6-ounce) jar marinated artichoke hearts, drained/quartered
½ cup pitted black olives, halved
¼ cup dry white wine (optional)
¼ teaspoon cinnamon
2¼ cups chicken broth
3 tablespoons margarine or butter
½ teaspoon salt (optional)
1½ cups quick-cooking couscous

Brown chicken in hot skillet with the oil. In a small bowl, stir together the tomatoes and soup mix; add to chicken in skillet. Bring to boiling, then reduce heat. Cover and simmer 30-45 minutes. Add artichokes, olives, wine (if using) and cinnamon. Simmer, covered, 10 minutes or until chicken is no longer pink inside.

Meanwhile, bring broth and margarine or butter to a boil in a saucepan. Add salt, if desired. Stir in couscous. Cover, remove from heat. Let stand 5 minutes. Fluff with a fork, and serve with chicken.

Creative Spirit

I am from stretched canvas and oil paints
a fan brush in my hand
a script brush waiting in silence
clenched between my teeth
Grumtine's citrus smell permeates my studio

I am from yeast dough and cinnamon
cold marble and peach cobblers
I'm from hardbacks and soft covers
lead pencils and spiral notebooks

From bolts of fabric stored in armoires
drawers and boxes of sewing notions
I thread my way through the patterns of life

I am from now but sleep with dead people
framed on my wall they tell me their secrets
keep me on branches of our family tree

Scraps of paper I own are valuable
birthdates or maiden names of obscure ancestors
dresses I've designed
poems I've scribbled while driving
recipes I've manipulated into gourmet delights
thumbnail sketches for paintings

I am of friendship and labor
clutter and chaos
excitement and frustration
desire and passion to create

I am from joy

White German Chocolate Cake will bring joy to your diners and test your creativity. The recipe is not difficult, but I save it for special events. It seems to take me a full morning to make it and leaves me with lots of dishes to do. But, it is SO worth it. In my opinion, this is a perfect celebration cake. Make sure you allow plenty of time to bake and assemble it. Serve it on a cake pedestal, if you have one. Not only is it delicious, it's a show-stopper.

White German Chocolate Cake

CAKE BATTER:
   8 ounces almond bark (white chocolate)
   ½ cup boiling water
   2 cups granulated sugar
   1 cup butter
   4 eggs, separated
   1 teaspoon vanilla
   2½ cups flour
   2 teaspoons baking powder
   ½ teaspoon salt
   1 cup buttermilk
   ½ cup pecans, chopped
   ½ cup flaked coconut

Preheat oven to 350°. Grease and flour three 9-inch cake pans.

In top of double boiler, melt chocolate in boiling water; set aside to cool.

In large mixing bowl, cream sugar and butter. Add egg yolks, one at a time, beating well after each addition. Stir in cooled chocolate and vanilla.

Sift flour, baking powder, and salt together three times; add to the cake mixture alternately with buttermilk. Beat egg whites until soft peaks form, and fold into the cake mixture. Add nuts and coconut.

Pour mixture into pans and bake for 30-35 minutes. Remove pans from oven; cool for five minutes, then remove cake layers to a cooling rack.

(See next page for topping, filling, and frosting recipes.)

White German Chocolate Cake (continued)

TOPPING AND FILLING:
- 1 cup sugar
- ½ cup Half and Half cream
- ¼ cup butter
- 1 teaspoon light corn syrup
- 1 teaspoon vanilla
- 1 cup pecans
- 1 cup coconut

In a 2-quart heavy saucepan, stir together all seven ingredients. After sugar is dissolved, boil 8-10 minutes. Let cool.

Spread mixture between cake layers and on top of cake.

FROSTING:
- 3 ounces cream cheese
- ½ cup butter
- 3 cups powdered sugar
- 1 teaspoon vanilla

Melt cream cheese and butter in a double boiler; remove from heat. Add powdered sugar and vanilla; beat until smooth. Frost sides of cake.

Election Day Is Coming

It's so close to the election, we can sum up the days on our fingers
We've been blasted with ads by promise-makers and a few mud-slingers

Candidates used to make speeches after they jumped up on tree stumps
Pretty easy back then to know who were honest and who were chumps

This season, with such a large cast of men and women running,
Should we vote for old country boys, ladies quite stunning, or someone more cunning

With media polls and phone surveys clamoring for our choices
It's time to allow the election board to record our private voices

The studious and informed will pick and choose when they cast their vote
While staunch supporters make bold checkmarks entirely by rote

Choosing our leaders is one of our freedoms, it's true
So if you want to stay free, it really is up to you

When election day dawns and we see results of campaigns mounted
Make sure that November Tuesday contains your ballot to be counted

Nothing says election or freedom like America and nothing says America better than apple pie.

Choose tart and firm apples for apple pie, such as Winesap or Jonathan. Use Granny Smith apples for a green apple pie.

Although pastry crusts have changed over the years, apple pies have been served daily in New England since 1630 when they were first referred to as "pyes" and sometimes topped with cream or cheese. Occasionally, they baked grated cheese inside the pie.

Apple Pie

1 cup granulated sugar
1 teaspoon cinnamon
¼ teaspoon nutmeg
6 cups peeled and sliced apples (Golden Delicious or Winesap)
1½ tablespoon butter
2-crust pastry for 9" pie
1 teaspoon sanding or granulated sugar (for top crust)

Preheat oven to 425°. Peel, core, and slice apples to ¼-inch slices. Place apple slices in a large bowl. In a small cup, combine 1 cup sugar and cinnamon; add to apple slices and stir gently. Pour mixture into bottom of pastry-lined pie pan; dot with butter. Cover with top crust; seal and flute edges. With a sharp knife, cut slits in top crust to vent. Sprinkle 1 teaspoon sugar over top of pie.

Bake 50-60 minutes or until apples are tender and crust is lightly browned. Remove from oven; let cool on a wire rack.

May be served warm or cold and topped with ice cream.

Variation: **Green Apple Pie**
Substitute Granny Smith apples and increase granulated sugar to 1½ cups; omit nutmeg.

The Shadow of Fear

Fear stalks me
Visits me in inky darkness
Filters into sun-dappled meadows
Howls above winter's wind
Creeps under moonlight's cast
Seduces fragile relationships
Hides in charcoal shadows
Encloses itself in mail
Encases innocent packages
Surrounds me and my world
Invades my personal space
Bides its time
Waits in the depths of insanity
Insinuates itself into my day
Infiltrates my conversations
Slithers in silence on its belly
Lulls me into false security
Strikes when I am most vulnerable
Grips my tattered soul
Refuses to disappear

Take the fear out of biscuit-making with this recipe for light, fluffy biscuits. They're good for any meal.

Angel Biscuits

1 package dry yeast
¼ cup warm water
2½ cups flour
¼ cup sugar
1 teaspoon baking powder
1 teaspoon salt
½ cup vegetable shortening, plus shortening to grease pan
1 cup buttermilk

Preheat oven to 400°. Grease pie pan or small cake pan with shortening.

Dissolve yeast in warm water; set aside. Combine flour, sugar, baking powder and salt in mixing bowl; cut in shortening. Stir in buttermilk and yeast mixture; blend thoroughly. Knead lightly on floured board, roll out on board, or just pat with open palm, and cut dough into biscuits with biscuit cutter or a floured drinking glass. Place biscuits into pan and let rise. Bake until browned on top.

Angels without Wings

Intense quacking of ducks in my neighbor's pond interrupts my Sunday afternoon nap and my dream of angels. One angel in the moonlight had lost her wing, the feathered structure making no sound as it drifted down through a sky of soft blue and into pure white clouds, puffed like meringue on cream pies. The angel's wing disappeared from my view just as the loud quacks woke me.

I shade my eyes from the sun to see four ducks lift off from the center of the pond and, while three of them fly without cause for concern, one struggles and cries out. His wings flap uncontrollably and I see he's lost a portion of one wing. Perhaps, it fell into the brushy woods nearby before he took flight. With quiet reserve and a severe lack of grace, he continues in flight, following his companions. Recognizing his plight, they reduce their speed. That's how it is with friendship.

When I became crippled, my true friends did not turn away. Although busy people with hectic life styles, they assisted me, when their schedules allowed, with moral support, a home-cooked meal or transportation to therapy. Their prayers allowed me to continue to live and to not give in to morbid thoughts and actions before I returned to work. Now, they sometimes slow their pace when we are together so that I may join them and participate in daily life.

I wonder if I were to search through the underbrush if I might find the duck's wingtip. Or, would it be like the fallen wing of my dream angel, floating in silence into eternity? I pray for the safety of the duck with his deformed wing and to thank God for the angel in my dream, giving me cause to again reflect on His living angels surrounding me.

Thank the earthbound angels in your life with this recipe for an angel food cake with texture so light you won't expect this much flavor.
Caution: You may never want to serve a store-bought angel food cake again. This recipe is easy to make; I like mine frosted with a powdered sugar icing but this cake stands alone, naked and delicious.

Angel Cake

10-12 egg whites (1½ cups), at room temperature
1½ teaspoon cream of tartar
1 teaspoon vanilla
1 cup sugar
1 cup all-purpose flour
1½ cups powdered sugar

In very large mixing bowl, beat egg whites, cream of tartar and vanilla with electric mixer on medium to high speed until *soft* peaks form. Gradually add sugar, about 2 tablespoons at a time, beating on medium to high speed until *stiff* peaks form.

Sift powdered sugar and flour together three times. Sift about ¼ of the dry mixture over beaten egg whites and gently fold in. Repeat sifting and folding steps, using ¼ of the flour mixture each time.

Pour batter evenly into an un-greased 10" tube pan. Gently cut through the cake batter with a knife or a narrow metal spatula. Bake on the lowest rack in a 350° oven for 40-45 minutes or until the top springs back when lightly touched. Immediately invert cake pan (over an empty glass pop or wine bottle) and cool completely. Using a narrow metal spatula or thin knife, loosen sides of cake from pan; then, remove cake from pan and place on a round cake plate or chop plate.

Slice cake and serve plain; dust it with powdered sugar; frost it with a fluffy white icing; or glaze it with a thin powdered-sugar frosting, tinted with food coloring for a pastel treat. It also makes a good substitute for shortcake, topped with strawberries or peaches.

Wash Monday

Morning began like any Monday
without rain.
An Oklahoma family prayed for relief
from drought in the southern plains,
did the wash,
hung clothes outside on a line.

Surprised to see a dark cloud
appear on the horizon,
they hoped it would bring rain by noon
and left the clothes to finish drying.

But, the cloud moved fast,
covering the whole sky,
choking out the sunlight.
No funnels formed. No sprinkles came.
But the noise – an insidious roar.

The parents herded their children inside,
closed up the house and watched huge insects
bang against windows.

Locusts ate everything green,
devoured tree leaves, crops and flowers,
left plant stalks only if they were brown.

Swarms attacked the wash on the clothesline.
Green and white gathered skirts
hung in shreds after giant grasshoppers
stripped them of their emerald stripes.
Locusts chewed sap green leaves and vines
from embroidered dresser scarves and chomped
viridian lace edgings crocheted on towels.

The pests left as quickly as they had come.

One thing my son Randy loves, any day of the week, is pancakes like his Grandma Dory always made – from scratch and with no recipe. I make a close second with this recipe. Serve crispy bacon or sausage on the side for breakfast or supper.

Favorite Pancakes

2 eggs
2½ cups whole milk
4 tablespoons vegetable oil
2½ cups flour
2½ tablespoons sugar
6 teaspoons baking powder
1 teaspoon salt
Vegetable shortening
Butter and Syrup

Mix eggs, milk, oil, flour, sugar, baking powder and salt together with a spoon in a large bowl; let sit 10 minutes. Melt vegetable shortening in a hot skillet; ladle a large spoonful of batter carefully into the hot grease and cook pancakes until brown on each side. Serve hot with butter and heated syrup.

Note: This makes a thinner pancake than the spongy ones in most restaurants but has much more taste, especially the crunchy edges. Pour heated, store-bought syrup over a buttered stack of pancakes. If you run out of syrup, make some. Refrigerate left-over batter to thin later with milk, or water, for great **Crepes**.

Quick Syrup

1 1/3 cups water
1 (1-pound) box light brown sugar
½ teaspoon butter
½ teaspoon vanilla

In a saucepan, bring water to a boil. Stir in sugar; boil until it starts to thicken. Stir in butter and vanilla. Serve hot.

Dusty Bowls

An Oklahoma family sat in silence
inside their closed farmhouse,
July's air humid and heavy,
thick as cold grits.

Through windows, fastened tight,
seams stuffed with rags,
they watched tumbleweeds skate by.
Red dirt swirled.

Little girls set the table,
turned plates and bowls upside down,
and helped bring food from the kitchen.

The father prayed for the wind to stop,
for soil to rest again on the ground.
When they opened their eyes,
they saw dirt had filtered in,
leaving a fine coat of dust on their old china.

My parents lived through the Depression and Dust Bowl eras in Oklahoma and set the table as depicted in the poem.

No southern cookbook would be complete without grits. This recipe sounds like holiday fare but, since we have canned pumpkin, it works for any time of the year.

Serve grits with roasted chicken and Brussels sprouts.

Pumpkin Grits

2/3 cup instant grits
1½ cups water
½ cup pumpkin puree
½ teaspoon salt
1 tablespoon fresh sage (optional)
1/3 cup shredded cheddar cheese

Bring water and to boil in a saucepan. Stir in grits, gradually, until combined. Stir in pumpkin, salt, and sage; return to a boil, then reduce heat to a simmer. Cook, uncovered, 5-4 minutes, or until the thickness you desire. Remove from heat; stir in cheese.

The Auction

A yellow orb rises in the east to greet me,
promising a clear October day.
At ten, a crowd gathers and gawks
while a woman of eighty-one summers
holds court on the green lawn of her gray house.
Her children and siblings surround her,
joined by neighbors and friends,
collectors and the curious.
They listen to a red-haired man cry the sale,
the same troublemaker
who rode the school bus she once drove.

No tears stain her cheeks
as they bid on her rock home.
Her personal treasures transfer to strangers.
She signs documents to relinquish ownership,
then lunches on junk food with relatives.

I return her to the Sleepy Hollow Home,
read her mail to her, reconcile her checkbook.
We reminisce the day away,
laughing about good years, remembering the sad.
We dine on meatloaf served on lap trays.
I polish her nails bright pink and leave.

A vibrant orange ball
slips low on the horizon.
Peach streaks decorate a pale lavender sky
until it darkens
and a silver moon beckons me home.

I call to let her know I'm safe,
my excuse for checking
to see if Mom's still coping.
We talk an hour to say goodnight
while darkness seals
one more chapter in our book of life.

Some auctions provide food booths or a food tent. Take along a sandwich if that's not the case and you plan to make a day of searching for bargains. This recipe makes four sandwiches.

Grilled Cheese and Apple Sandwiches

8 slices sturdy bread, sliced ½-inch thick
Mayonnaise or yellow mustard
6 ounces Gruyere cheese, sliced
8 ounces baked ham, sliced thin
2 Granny Smith apples
4 ounces Swiss cheese, sliced thin
Butter, softened to room temperature

Preheat an electric sandwich press. As an alternative, heat 2 iron skillets over medium heat for at least 2 minutes and have ready a foil-covered clean brick or other weight and hot pads. Skillets will be screaming-hot.

On four slices of bread, spread a thin coating of mayonnaise or mustard. Add Gruyere cheese and ham slices. (Ham is optional.)

Core, but do not peel, apples; slice thinly. Place apple slices on top of cheese and ham, use lots of apple slices. Top with Swiss cheese and remaining bread slices for 4 sandwiches. Butter the outside of top pieces of bread.

Place sandwiches in sandwich press; cover and cook 6-8 minutes. If using skillets, place 2 sandwiches, buttered side down, in one skillet. Spread butter on the outside of the top pieces of bread. Cover sandwich skillet with second skillet and weight it down with the brick. Cook until bread is toasted and cheese melts. Remove weight and top skillet. Move sandwiches to a wire rack to keep warm. Repeat process for remaining 2 sandwiches.

Serve immediately, Or, let cool and wrap individual sandwiches in foil for transport. Refrigerate extras.

Don't' Get Caught On the Bridge

Clack, clack, click, clack, clack.

Daddy's tires on the rusty Ford pickup ran over the long boards, weathered and curled on the edges. The old Raedeker Bridge had its signature sound, as all country bridges do. But, Raedeker's went on and on.

Clack, clack, click, clack, clack.

Five steel spans allowed cars and horses, as well as the occasional foot traveler, to cross the Cimarron River. Long steel bolts fastened tall beams together to form the huge structure, now rusty from years of exposure to the elements.

We drove across the bridge when the river seemed at peace. Beige sandbars lengthened the land, forcing the shallow Cimarron to wind like a slender red ribbon until it disappeared around a bend. In summer, weeds and grasses grew on the sandbars far below the bridge, making the hot stretch of sand a favored place for family picnics.

But, when Oklahoma's storm season produced mammoth buckets of rain each year, the sandbars dissolved into a wide river again. Red water ate away the chocolate-colored banks.

When the river flooded and covered the bridge, Daddy drove us across the Raedeker, the churning water up past our truck's front bumper. We remembered the old residents' cautions: "Drive slow. Don't stop. Or else, your engine will drown out."

We kids wanted to know: What if the water keeps rising and washes us away? What if the bridge gets washed away?

"That will never happen," they said. "But, don't get caught on the bridge."

Before depression-era laborers built the Raedeker, Bill Ricks brought my grandfather and his children across the river in a rowboat to work on his farm. My mother said they carried buckets and paring knives to pick cucumbers all day for fifteen cents a bushel. My Grandpa Hopkins helped build that bridge. On November 12, 1932, the same day his last child was born, Grandpa Hopkins carved the bridge's completion date into its north concrete abutment.

Years later, my brothers and I crossed the bridge often on our way to and from town and over to Grandpa's house to help him mow grass. As young teens, we fished in the river for catfish and perch and played on the wide sandbars. Sometimes, Grandpa would play softball with us and run the bases when he hit a home run, wearing a floppy hat on his bald head. He ran fast for an old codger in overalls and bare feet.

The river drew us to it when it flooded its banks. Tires and outhouses floated down; old rusty cars and dead cattle hung up under the bridge until they washed free and the raging water forced them farther downstream.

When the muddy water rose several inches inside their homes, we helped our neighbors move their furniture to dry ground. Daddy and Grandpa Hopkins worked well together, even though they were in-laws. They showed us how to pull Mr. Ricks' peanuts early to save them before the river covered his plants. Fish and snakes slithered over our feet and brushed our ankles when we picked his melons and cucumbers, submerged in the flood's backwaters. If we had time for play, we caught carp, catfish and goldfish with our hands. Goldfish, in an array of bright colors and more than a foot in length, swam between the plant rows, displaced by rising water that had flooded their ponds and streams.

Caramel-colored foam skimmed by from upriver, roiling in the turbulent water. The car radio announced how high the Cimarron crested in other towns above us; that's how we gauged the amount of time we had before the river would overflow its banks near the Raedeker and Daddy would give the signal to move our cars and trucks to higher ground.

Chicken houses skated by, one with a white rooster and two speckled hens on the peak of its roof, the only portion that stayed above water as it dipped and pitched. Experience taught us how to read the river and we compared each flood to the river marks left on the trunk of a giant oak tree at the road's edge near the bridge. We did until, one year, the river gobbled away so much bank that it stole our tree, our history.

Later, when the Raedeker Bridge groaned and twisted in the Flood of 1957 like a mighty iron giant in pain, it crashed into the demon water below. Four of its five spans pulled away and mired themselves in deep river sand, buried for eternity, the abutment and Grandpa's carving destroyed but his legacy intact.

Pan-Fried Catfish

1½ to 2 pounds catfish, cleaned and deboned
1½ cups cornmeal
½ cup flour
1 teaspoon seasoned salt
¼ teaspoon black pepper
1 cup buttermilk

In pie plates or shallow bowls, mix cornmeal, flour, seasoned salt, and pepper in one and pour buttermilk in another. Dip catfish fillets, or pieces, in buttermilk first and then in cornmeal mixture; coat well. Place fish on a wire rack.

Heat oil in a large skillet over medium heat; add catfish pieces but do not crowd. Fry 3-5 minutes per side, or until golden and fish flakes with a fork. Remove from skillet, keeping warm until all are cooked.

Serve with tartar sauce on the side. Cole slaw and a green vegetable complete the meal. Sometimes, you need French fries.

Shepherd Tartar Sauce

¼ cup horseradish mustard
¾ cup regular mayonnaise
2 tablespoons sweet pickle relish

In a small bowl, combine mustard, mayonnaise and sweet pickle relish; stir until mixed.

Serve beside baked fish, fried fish and seafood.

Note: This type of tartar sauce has a mild bite and seems to appeal to men. Recipe is easy to make in any amount due to its one-to-three formula – one part mustard to three parts mayonnaise; add as much relish as desired. It must be sweet pickles.

Modern-Day Horse Trader

an engine roars
a strange car pops into view
bounces over terraces
tops the third one and levels out
on the long sandy drive

is it company?

too close to suppertime for unannounced guests
I shade my eyes from the setting sun
strain to see what my father
drives home today from work

he would have made a fine horse trader in cowboy days

dressed in blue denim overalls, he left at dawn
silver hard hat and black lunch bucket in hand
driving a blue Ford coupe

his face now blackened
by ten hard hours at the refinery
he looks good in the green sedan
his eyes sparkle
he glides to a stop in a Packard with suicide doors

I wonder how long we'll keep it

No one carries that black or silver lunchbox with a hinged lid any more in today's world. We rely on restaurants and fast food chains. If we do pack a lunch from home, most of us can heat it up in a microwave at the office or plant. For shift workers, breakfast fare may be preferred.

Breakfast Burritos

12 (or more) strips of bacon
12 eggs
Salt and pepper
10 (8-inch) flour tortillas
1½ cups shredded cheddar cheese
2 green onions, sliced into thin rounds
Mayonnaise (optional)

Cook bacon in a large skillet until crisp; remove from skillet to drain on paper towels. Pour bacon grease into heatproof cup. Return 2 tablespoons to skillet; save remainder to season beans, etc.

In a bowl, whisk eggs with salt and pepper; pour into hot skillet with burner set on medium-low heat. Stir and cook until eggs are set but not dry. Remove from heat.

Working on waxed paper, lay out tortillas. Spread cooked eggs down the middle of each tortilla, dividing eggs evenly. Crumble cooked bacon and divide among tortillas; sprinkle with onion slices. Fold bottom and sides of each tortilla over filling to make burritos.

Serve immediately.

To save for lunches, wrap each burrito in waxed paper and aluminum foil; freeze.

At lunchtime, remove foil from frozen burrito; leave wrapped in waxed paper. Microwave until heated through; let stand 30 seconds.

Variation: Substitute cooked sausage for bacon, but scramble eggs in butter instead of sausage drippings. You can also substitute Colby and Monterey Jack cheese for the cheddar.

Pioneer Stone Masons

The Hopkins' boys could lay red brick all day,
cooked their own mortar in open fire pits,
but they were more gifted craftsmen than that.
The three young Kansans were true stone masons
when they brought their trade south before statehood.
They dug massive boulders from dark red earth,
chipping and carving them into large squares.
They raised those heavy stones with trusty mules,
stacked and wedged them into two-story houses.
The men are gone but their houses remain,
standing strong against Oklahoma's sky,
survivors of fierce winds and brutal storms.

Although they mixed and cooked their own mortar, they built some homes without it. Two single-story homes sit side-by-side and are still in use in Cushing, Oklahoma. For those, the men dry-fit stones they had shaped with care – flat stones in multi-colors and only a couple of inches in height.

Using larger stones and brick they had made, the men built nearly all of the business buildings on downtown Main Street in early-day Cushing.

They had been farmers in Pennsylvania before moving to Kansas where they farmed and learned the stonemason trade. They came to Oklahoma shortly after the run in 1893, settling in northern Lincoln County. Later, they moved to Payne County – two of them to Cushing, where they continued their trade, and the third to south of Ripley where he resumed farming. They built his two-story home of large sandstone boulders; it has been nominated for the National Register of Historic Places.

My mother always made this candy; no recipe existed. Her cousins, a family of all boys who stayed at home while their parents worked in the early 1930's, cooked for themselves and concocted this special treat. They shared their creation with my mother and she made it for almost seventy years. With only three ingredients, we didn't need a recipe until a cookbook committee requested it for publication more than a decade ago.

Potato Candy – Hopkins

1 very small potato, peeled and diced
1 (16-ounce) box powdered sugar
Peanut Butter

Boil potato in water in a small saucepan until tender. Drain potato, reserving water. Mash potato with a fork; add powdered sugar; mix until thick enough to roll out; adding a few drops of the reserved water, if necessary. Discard the remaining water. Using powdered sugar like flour, dust a rolling pin and pastry board. Roll out dough; spread with peanut butter; roll up jelly-roll fashion, using a thin spatula to lift dough when it sticks to the board. Slice into ½-inch round pinwheels and place on waxed paper until pieces are dry and set. Store candy in a covered container.

My son, Randy, loves potato candy almost as much as he does pralines. He adored his Grandma Dory whom we saw as often as we could although we never lived close by. On every trip to his grandparents' home, Randy could count on her special pancakes. She made potato candy for him when he was pretty young, but he remembers that visit with Grandma Dory well. He laughs now and says, "On <u>one</u> visit, that woman got me hooked on potato candy, Dr. Pepper®, and Dentyne® gum."

Butterfly Garden

Although it's autumn,
I watch a parade of butterflies
fly in and fold their wings
to drink nectar from new blooms of red, yellow
and magenta zinnias. Then, the winged beauties congregate
on huge coneflowers of faded cream and lavender.
The flower bed is a tangle of survivors from past weedings,
the last blooming stalks now drooping and turning brown.

I didn't plan a butterfly garden this year – just flowers
to complement my hibiscus and a few rosebushes.
What came were colors so vibrant everyone noticed them
while whizzing by on the street – you could hear
their engines slow for a better view.
Enjoying the riot of color most were those religious
with their morning jog and those who strolled by
every evening on my curved sidewalk.
Planting only from seed, I watched all varieties
reach for the sky. Coneflowers advertised
to reach three feet attained six and seven.
I'm glad I didn't fertilize because
what should have been eighteen-inch zinnias tripled in size.
Dwarf marigolds exploded into borders of yellow, orange
and burgundy – two feet taller than predicted.

I'll go out soon, with clippers, to snip dry heads
and save paper-thin petals of seed, though I
may not need to sow in spring – so much has already fallen,
implanting itself for next year's display and butterfly feast.
I'll pull out all the giant stalks to make a flat bed
for the blankets of snow coming this winter.

Autumn brings apples in various colors and degrees of sweetness. Piled in a plain bowl, apples can decorate your dining table, their natural beauty as pleasing as a bouquet of flowers. A long line of green apples on a simple, weathered board adds a welcoming touch to your kitchen counter or windowsill..

Applesauce Cake

2½ cups flour
1 teaspoon baking soda
1½ teaspoon baking powder
1 teaspoon ground cinnamon
½ teaspoon ground cloves
Pinch salt
½ cup butter
2 cups granulated sugar
2 eggs, beaten
½ cup chopped nuts
½ cup hot water
1¾ cup cold applesauce

Heat oven to 350°.
Have ready a greased and floured 13x9-inch cake pan.
Sift flour, baking soda, baking powder, cinnamon, cloves, and salt together two times; set aside.
In the mixing bowl of an electric mixer, cream butter; add sugar gradually and cream together until light and fluffy. Beat in eggs and nuts.
Adding a small amount at a time to the bowl, beat in part of the dry ingredients, alternating with the hot water and then with the applesauce. Beat after each addition and end with the dry ingredients. Beat until smooth. Pour batter into prepared pan.
Bake for 1 hour. Remove from oven and let cool.

Bare Feet

sand beneath my feet
gritty and hot
I long for ice water and shade
to quench my thirst and cool my soles

shoes are for school and church
bare feet for hoeing truck patches
and this cotton field

night bath in number two wash tub
asphalt tile cool to my feet
makes it all worthwhile
until daylight
when the fields again call my name

I loved school, partly because I could learn new things plus I didn't have so much hoeing to do. Chores were year round, but the cold seasons didn't require daily labor like summertime. Fall meant clearing trees for pasture, and winter meant burning brush piles and bringing in wood for the stove.

Speaking of school, my elementary school made great lunches for grades 1-6. Since we had no lunchroom at the high school building, students in grades 7-12 could walk four blocks downtown to eat a quick lunch from our two cafes. Most students walked four blocks in the other direction to eat at the elementary school where the food was good and the price was cheap. Not many students had cars, so some caught a ride but most walked no matter the weather. A favorite treat from grade school was a spicy cookie, large and square. When I graduated from high school, one of the cooks gave me the recipe. Mrs. Grantham wrote it out. Although it stated how to mix the dough, it didn't say how to shape the dough for chilling, how to bake the cookies, or how much spice to add. I've added more instructions and hope you like these as much as I did.

Ice Box Cookies

6 cups flour
4 teaspoons baking powder
½ teaspoon salt
1 teaspoon cinnamon
1½ cups shortening
3 cups brown sugar, packed
1 cup granulated sugar
4 eggs, well beaten
2 teaspoons vanilla

Sift flour, baking powder, salt, and cinnamon. Set aside.
Cream shortening and sugars until fluffy, add eggs and vanilla; mix well. Add dry ingredients and mix well.
Shape into a square log, wrap in waxed paper, and chill for several hours. Slice log into cookies ¼-½-inch thick, place on cookie sheet, and bake at 350° for 10-12 minutes. Let cookies cool on pan for a minute, then transfer them to a cooling rack.

Variation: Can add other spices or, instead of spices, add chocolate, nuts, dried fruit, or coconut to dough before chilling.

Freedom

We fly the red, white and blue,
symbols of American pride,
in our yards,
on our houses
and from our cars.
We wear flag pins on our chests.

We watch city celebrations,
free from tyranny and persecution.
We let our children ride bikes, tricycles
and scooters in neighborhood parades
while new mothers push babies in strollers,
unencumbered by terror.

We bake holiday treats and walk down sidewalks
to deliver them, safe from explosions and stray bullets.
Our nation celebrates freedom each year on the Fourth of July,
but we live it every day.

Celebrate freedom and all patriotic holidays with everything red, white, and blue – flags, parades, flower bouquets, party decorations, cakes, ice cream, and more.

Patriotic Ice Cream

1 (10-ounce) package frozen strawberries
½ cup sugar
2/3 cup heavy cream

In a food processor, combine frozen strawberries and sugar; process until berries are coarsely-chopped. With processor running on low speed, pour heavy cream in slowly; process until it is fully incorporated.

Serve immediately for a soft-serve version of "red" ice cream. Serve in individual bowls or atop ice cream cones. Place in freezer for a harder consistency. Will keep in freezer a few weeks.

Variations:

Substitute frozen blueberries for the strawberries for "blue" ice cream.

For "white" ice cream, substitute one frozen banana for the strawberries; add a crushed vitamin C tablet to prevent browning.

Valley of Sinful People

Temperance strained to hear conversation from the living room. She hated the banishment of all children when the adults' tempers flared. That was when she and her sister Charity could learn more of the outside world, times when the adults spoke of evil and sinful ways of those people who lived just over the mountain.

She had made it to the top of that mountain one glorious day, like today. But this time, golden slivers of sun glinted on the silver scissors Temperance carried. Log homes, chinked with mud and ash, peppered the valley below and stared up at her, teasing her, testing her resolve. Would she cross over the ridge and stumble down its rugged wall to appease her curiosity? What were those people like, those families who lived in the same land but practiced foreign ways?

No, Temperance decided. Twelve was too young to venture into the unknown. She saw children playing around a maypole, their laughter carried up to her on the wind, soft music to her ears. Her father would swing the strap against her behind if she left their side of the mountain, and maybe because she climbed to the ridge again today. But, she didn't care.

Her hands, steady as when she embroidered flowers and crosses on quilt blocks, pressed the scissors against the long braid that lay heavy on her neck and touched her waist in the front. She held her braid in one hand, away from her starched white collar, and cut it free with her other hand, the one holding her mother's silver shears. Sharp though they were, it took a while for her to saw through the thick dark braid, shiny and healthy from years of 200 nightly strokes.

When her braid fell limp in her hand, she untied its tail and pulled it apart in long, thin wisps and let the wind carry it down the mountain where the sinful people lived. She wished she could follow it down. She could tell Father that she had to retrieve her hair. Neatness and putting things away he would understand. But no, she decided she was too young for the adventure and her search for answers. Maybe she would follow her hair next year, Temperance decided, when she would turn thirteen.

For a sinfully-rich dessert, try this frozen torte. Make it the day ahead and prepare the sauce just prior to serving.

Ice Cream Torte with Berries and Chocolate Sauce

CRUST:
>½ cup chocolate wafers, finely crushed
>1 tablespoon sugar
>1 tablespoon egg white, slightly beaten
>Cooking spray

Preheat oven to 350°. Coat a 9-inch spring-form pan with cooking spray. Combine cookie crumbs, sugar and egg white in a small bowl; toss with a fork until moist. Press mixture into bottom and up sides of pan. Bake 15 minutes; remove from oven and cool on a wire rack.

FILLING:
>6 cups vanilla ice cream, slightly softened
>3 cups strawberry or raspberry sherbet, slightly-softened
>2 tablespoons semi-sweet chocolate mini-chips

Spread 3 cups ice cream into cooled crust; cover with plastic wrap; freeze until firm. Spread sherbet over ice cream in crust; freeze again until firm. Spread remaining 3 cups ice cream over sherbet; sprinkle with mini-chips. Freeze until firm.

SAUCE:
>1 cup water
>1 cup granulated sugar
>½ cup dark corn syrup
>1 ounce bittersweet chocolate, grated
>¼ cup cocoa
>¼ cup evaporated milk
>2 teaspoons vanilla
>Strawberries or Raspberries

Bring water, sugar, and syrup to a boil in a small saucepan over medium heat; reduce heat to low and simmer mixture until slightly thick (about 15 minutes.) Remove from heat; add chocolate and cocoa; whisk until smooth. Stir in milk and vanilla.

To serve: Spoon warm sauce over slices of frozen torte; garnish each serving with whole berries.

China Painters

a single rose emerges
petal by delicate petal
on ivory porcelain

each brushstroke by skillful artisans,
deft, premeditated, loving,
brings velvety blooms to life
glossy leaves of viridian and amarillo
surround pale crimson buds
pastel teal and violet fronds
feather into the background

twigs and thorns dance on graceful pitchers,
sturdy enough to carry wine and water,
life's necessary liquids,
yet fragile like the rose,
rare beauties until spent
and whisked away by the wind

Whether you pour Champagne Punch from a delicate porcelain pitcher or serve it from an elegant punch bowl, you'll enjoy the compliments.

Champagne Punch

1 quart cranberry juice cocktail
4 (6 ounce) or 2 (12-ounce) cans frozen lemonade, undiluted
2 (12-ounce) cans frozen orange juice, undiluted
4 (46-ounce) cans pineapple juice
1 or 2 fifths Champagne [*2 works best*]
3 quarts ginger ale
2 quarts club soda

Mix juices and champagne together; add ginger ale and club soda. Serve chilled.

Serves 115 guests in 4-ounce punch cups.

Variation: Wine may be used in place of Champagne.

(Note: For serving, try an additional can of frozen orange juice, thawed and diluted with water, then re-frozen into a ring to keep punch chilled.)

White Silk

a breeze blew into Laticia's room
billowed sheer lace curtains
danced them across her bed
tall, dark cherry spikes
of a four-poster pierced the room
austere in its whiteness
its nothingness
a harsh environment
except for silk sheets
and a heavy scent of honeysuckle
carried on the air
warmed by an afternoon sun
Laticia woke from a nap
stretched her long ebony legs
white silk draped her
drifted to the floor
seductive in its innocence

*White, seductive, and feels like silk to your tongue describes a candy so divine, it's called **Divinity**.*

My mother made perfect divinity every time. On the next page, I shared her method which differs from other recipes out there. For holidays, we made at least three batches, coloring two of them with food coloring, to give us white, pink, and pastel green candies.

Divinity

2½ cups granulated sugar
½ cup corn syrup
½ cup water
2 egg whites
½ teaspoon vanilla
Pecans or Walnuts, chopped

Combine sugar, syrup and water in a heavy saucepan; cook to thin syrup stage; remove from heat. Beat egg whites in mixer bowl. Slowly pour one third of syrup mixture over egg whites, beating constantly. Cook remaining syrup until it spins a thread; remove from heat. Pour half of this mixture slowly over egg whites, beating constantly. Cook remaining syrup to hardball stage (250°-268°); remove from heat and pour slowly over egg whites. Beat well; mix in vanilla and nuts; drop by teaspoon onto waxed paper. Let cool and store in a covered container. (Keeps for at least two weeks.)

Life's Thread

Slender threads weave
throughout my soul
Tender threads of love
He lavishes and makes me whole

Silver threads grace my scalp
while wrinkles line my face
until a star twinkles
and God prepares my place

Grandparents, aunts and uncles, cousins and more distant relatives migrated to our farm home almost every Sunday at noon for a big dinner when I was a child. We ate Mom's great cooking, always topped off with marvelous desserts. We spent the afternoon visiting and playing cards, and sometimes playing a game of softball out on Bermuda grass. No family get-together was considered complete until Mom made a big pan, or two, of candy. The Hopkins clan loved anything sweet and chocolate fudge was a given, the thread that kept our family connected. Mom and Grandma Hopkins knew how to make everything, even candy, without a recipe. Here's my adaptation for one recipe that was never written down.

Hopkins Fudge

3 cups granulated sugar
3 heaping tablespoons cocoa
½ cup water
1 cup Milnot® (evaporated milk)
Dash salt
1½ sticks butter
1½ teaspoons vanilla
Pecans or Walnuts, if desired

Butter 2 dinner plates with additional butter; set aside.

Combine sugar and cocoa in a heavy pot. Add water, milk, salt and all but 2 teaspoons of the butter; mix with spoon; cook, stirring occasionally, until softball stage when a few drops of mixture dropped into a small cup of very cold water forms a soft ball which flattens when removed from the water, or 234°. Remove from heat; add remaining 2 teaspoons butter and vanilla but do not stir. Let cool to almost lukewarm; beat vigorously with a large spoon until mixture thickens and loses its gloss; quickly stir in nuts. Pour candy into buttered plates. Let cool and cut into squares.

Among the Folds

Kitchen towels line up like soldiers,
draped over handles of oven doors.
Memories hide among the folds.

Company waits to devour holiday's dinner,
discussing their place in genealogy, among the folds.

Diners pack the feast in tightly to tummies big and small,
slathering butter on croissants among the folds.

Grandma's belly rests on her thighs;
not much lap left among the folds.

Grandpa sports several chins.
When he laughs, they wiggle like jelly among the folds.

Grandchildren line up for hugs and new quilts from Grandma.
They snuggle into the folds.

The crowd takes leftovers home and disappears.
Grandma dries dishes with her new towels
before her tears fall into the folds.

My grandmother on my mother's side was a good cook who never needed recipes, but I wasn't able to spend time with her in her kitchen where I could have learned a lot. I have a couple recipes from my father's stepmother. Others lived far away. Mom was a fabulous cook but said she didn't have the patience to teach me – that I would learn how to cook in home economics. Over the years, those classes changed.

She learned the basics of cooking, as basic as instructions on how to make toast. My class spent little time on cooking; we learned how to cook baked beans and popovers. Mom did teach me how to make peanut butter cookies, but other than that, I had to learn how to cook on my own after I moved away to find work.

For this book, I've written how-to instructions, except for the Ghoulash recipe below. I wanted to include a recipe that shows you how most of my recipes that I've accumulated over the years have been written – no amounts and no directions. I learned to cook anyway, and if you're new to cooking, you can too with the recipes in this book. Happy Cooking to you!

Ghoulash

Hamburger Meat   Macaroni
Tomatoes   Onions
Salt & Pepper   Garlic Salt
Heinz 57   Catsup & Water
Tomato Sauce

Compass for Life

Maria's yard leads me back to nature. An April sun, warm and serene, invites me into a pleasant morning, a rare day with no prairie wind and quiet enough to hear the chatter of birds. Only the roar of engines interrupts the peace when vehicles blaze by on a county road. A gentle breeze tickles the soft leaves of new ivy embroidering stately trunks on a stand of oak trees. One of the trees bears scars of abuse from years ago, its burls a reminder of how man's desires redirected the oak's growth. But, the delay does not diminish its beauty. Destined for redemption, the burls provide inspiration for a master craftsman to create fine furniture.

In today's fast-paced world, we seldom take time to enjoy nature, the ebb and flow of birth, maturity and death. When plants die, they provide protection for new shoots to emerge and fill the void left by faded blooms and dried leaves. What do we leave when we die? Are we cognizant of our pending legacy? Do we live our lives as a testimonial for actions that brought us fame or fortune? Or, do we encourage others, not to follow in our footsteps, but to stand on our shoulders and reach for something higher, something to better their lives and to call their own?

A moment alone in our own backyards grounds us, lets nature revisit and refresh our souls. Free for us to enjoy and cherish comes the gift of nature, created and embellished by God.

Embellish these cookies for any season with colored icing, sprinkles, nuts, mini-chips, etc. Let the kids help decorate them.

Sugar Cookies

½ cup butter
½ cup margarine
½ cup granulated sugar
½ cup powdered sugar
½ teaspoon baking soda
½ teaspoon cream of tartar
½ teaspoon salt
1½ teaspoon vanilla
1 egg, beaten
2½ cups flour

Preheat oven to 375°.
Butter or grease baking sheet with shortening.
Cream butters and sugars together. Add soda, cream of tartar, salt and vanilla. Stir in egg and flour. Shape into balls and flatten or roll out and use cookie cutters. Place on baking sheet and bake for 10 minutes. Remove from pan to cool.

The Necklace

A shiny conch shell
out of water decorates
sweet Maria's chest.

Conch Shells

Seashells exemplify strength and beauty in nature, especially the conch. God designs these gifts, always in proportion, whether as large as a cat or as tiny as a thumb. They provide a home for God's other creatures, carried on soft currents, tossed about in storms, and scattered on white beaches. When the conch fulfills its primary purpose, it continues its journey from littered castaway to decorative ornament – large ones to grace our coffee tables or mantels, small ones cozy in a corner of our china cabinets.

If we mortals move to a new home, we seldom discard the conch, its delicate markings like ivory stripes on peach porcelain. Although it costs us nothing to acquire, we treat the little shells like heirlooms, valued enough to admire daily, then to pass on to our dearest friends and relatives.

When we complete our purpose in life and pass on, our bodies leave shells that do not retain the enduring beauty of sea shells. That's why we must strive for enrichment and values that transcend our time here on earth. To touch another person's soul in a way that brings him joy or peace, when tossed about on *his* journey, is the invisible shell that we can leave behind – litter on the sands of life.

When it comes to protein in a shell, shrimp is my favorite. Serve this quick fix as an entrée or on a buffet table as an appetizer. (Peel shrimp after cooking for appetizer.)

Skillet Shrimp

2 pounds raw shrimp
2 tablespoons butter
1 tablespoon ground black pepper blend
1 teaspoon crushed dried rosemary leaves
1¼ cups Italian salad dressing
Fresh rosemary or parsley, for garnish
Lemon wedges

Wash and clean shrimp, removing heads but leaving shells and tails on; set aside.

In a large skillet, mix butter, pepper, rosemary leaves, and salad dressing; heat to boiling. Add the shrimp; cook until boiling while stirring constantly for 6 minutes. Shrimp should turn pink.

Spoon shrimp and liquid into individual serving bowls; garnish with fresh herbs.

Serve with lemon wedges and hard rolls.

Chimes

Oriental chimes are touted as soothing, peaceful. They let your mind and body become one to allow meditation on an individual level. Perhaps, I'm never at peace, my thoughts too jumbled to meditate. My mind and body are in a constant tug of war.

When I entered the room designated for my writing group, I was excited to try a new writing exercise and a shared experience where we learn from one another. Sometimes, a writer pours out her soul on paper and we applaud her courage.

Instead, I walked into a somber room where loud chimes assailed me before disturbing tones attacked my brain. It was similar to another time when we tried to write with loud chanting that surrounded us.

Each of us has her own strengths and weaknesses, her own needs, fears, and desires. I used to wish for peace and solitude when my life was loud and chaotic. But, if I lived in a meditative world of Oriental chiming, I doubt that peace would linger long with me.

Instead, meet me at the nearest café where I write amidst the clatter of dishes, the din of diners, the smell of grease, and the murmur of lovers. That's what chimes for me.

There's nothing better than a fried hamburger at a "greasy spoon," although you need to choose a good and clean café where they fry, instead of grill, their burgers. Don't skip their hand-cut French fries and onion rings made from scratch – never frozen. They can't be beat.

French-Fried Onion Rings

Large Spanish or Bermuda onions
Flour, for dry-coating onions
Vegetable oil, for frying

BATTER:
1 cup flour
1 teaspoon baking powder
½ teaspoon salt
1 egg
1 cup milk
¼ cup vegetable oil

Peel onions, as many as you'd like; cut crosswise into 1/4 –inch thick slices and separate into rings. Pat dry with paper towels. Place onions in a large plastic bag with flour; seal and shake.

Make batter. In a small bowl, combine 1 cup flour, baking powder, and salt; set aside. In another small bowl, combine egg, milk, and 1/3 cup vegetable oil; whisk until blended. Add dry ingredients; whisk until batter is smooth.

Heat 2 inches oil in a frying pan or large saucepan. While it heats, remove a few of the floured rings from plastic bag. Use tongs to make it easier. Dip rings into the batter. Remove from batter, letting excess batter drip back into the bowl. Carefully drop battered onion rings into the hot oil; fry a few at a time for 2 minutes or so. Rings should be golden, not quite brown. Remove from heat; let drain on paper towel-lined platter. Sprinkle with salt and keep cooked onion rings warm while you fry the remainder.

Serve warm with ketchup, ranch dressing, spicy sauces, etc.

Ponder Time

The first rain of spring patters soft drops on my old barn roof. I sit in the loft on top of last summer's prairie hay, fingering the dried twine that still imprisons the bales, and wonder where I will be when haying season comes again. Will I wear leather gloves and grip a long steel hook to heave the bales onto a flatbed trailer, or will the ancient round-baler give out this time?

Having seen sixty years of faithful service, the rusty machine surprises me every summer when it follows my tractor and spits out perfectly-tied, 45-pound cylinders of green prairie grasses. Alone, I can manage these small bales for my cattle and one good horse, but when the baler chooses to retire, I'll have to sell the farm. I can't afford new equipment and the round balers of today shoot out monster bales that only forklifts, or hay spikes mounted on pickup beds, can maneuver. I could pay someone to bale for me, but I wouldn't be able to load the big hay and move it around to feed my livestock.

Maybe it's time for me to hang up my hay hook, move into town and retire from ranching, but that's all I know. And, that's all I want to do. Where else could I sit and smell hay and the freshness of rain while I remember how it used to be when my whole family lived at home and danced outside in wet clothes in spring's first shower?

Like the beef stockman in this story, you should have plenty of time to ponder when you make something in your slow cooker.

Beef and Vegetable Soup   (12-24 hours)

STEP 1:

 2 pounds beef shank, short ribs, or oxtails
 2 quarts water
 1 onion, chopped
 2 carrots, chopped
 2 celery stalks, chopped
 1 cup tomatoes, diced
 1 cub cabbage, shredded (optional)
 2 tablespoons salt
 5 whole peppercorns
 1 tablespoons sugar
 1 bay leaf

Combine all ingredients in slow cooker; cover and cook on Low for 12 hours. Remove beef from soup and trim meat from bones. Dice meat and return it to soup mixture in slow cooker.

STEP 2:

 1 cup (3/4 pound) fresh or frozen peas, thawed
 1 cup (3/4 pound) fresh or frozen green beans, thawed

Add peas and beans to slow cooker. Cover and cook on High for 1½ -2 hours or on Low for 12 more hours.

(Note: For a darker broth, brown the meat in a hot oven before placing in the slow cooker, or stir in 1 tablespoon Kitchen Bouquet or brown gravy extract before serving.)

Scars

You stripe my body
like a zebra's coat gone awry

New red lines intersect old white ones
crisscross newer ones still shiny
all widths, all lengths
each with a story to tell

Some surgeries I breezed through
Others nearly took my life

Yet I breathe and walk
wearing my patchwork skin

Don't let anything scare you. Let the word "chicken" describe the delicious poultry dishes you prepare in your kitchen.

Basic Fried Chicken

1 cup flour
1 (3-4 pound) chicken, cut up
Shortening
1 teaspoon salt
½ teaspoon black pepper
1½ cups milk (for gravy)

Put flour in a paper lunch sack or a large plastic bag. Place chicken pieces, a few at a time, into bag and shake. Remove pieces; place on waxed paper. Reserve remaining flour for gravy.

In a very large skillet over medium-high heat, melt enough shortening to cover bottom of skillet with about ½ inch of grease. Add chicken pieces; sprinkle with salt and pepper; fry until browned on all sides. Reduce heat to low; cover skillet and cook 30 minutes. Remove cover and increase heat to medium; cook 2-3 minutes or until chicken can be moved with coating intact. Turn pieces and cook an additional 2-3 minutes until pieces are crisp all around. Remove from skillet to a warm platter.

Make pan gravy by draining away all but 2 tablespoons grease. Add 2 tablespoons flour and brown, stirring to loosen fond. Gradually add the milk and bring to a boil; cook and stir for a couple minutes until gravy thickens. Season with salt and pepper. Pour gravy into a bowl or gravy boat to serve with chicken.

Fragile Photographs

At a yard sale, I stand in a long line with a group of strangers, all of us looking for bargains among the remnants of some poor soul's life. None of us knew the decedent whose items had been put up for auction in another state. What didn't sell at the estate auction made its way into large plastic bins and traveled to our town in the back of a scavenger's pickup. The junk dealer makes a living from holding garage, yard and tag sales for others, charging a percentage of the total sales. It's a necessary job for those too busy or too crippled to hold their own events, but when the dealers finish selling the furniture, jewelry and guns and get down to the photographs and mementos, they seem more like vultures, tearing apart visual memories that touched someone's heart and helped them through a tough time, brought a tear of joy to a wrinkled cheek, or held an old-timer's sanity intact. Although these are pieces of old paper, they contain memories so powerful they can evoke passionate emotions in seasoned shoppers – like us.

A portion of a wedding party, circa 1930's, peers up at me from a sepia print. Three young women in floor-length lace dresses and elegant hats, with sheer wide brims, hold bridesmaid's bouquets. And, the flower girl with them, dressed in tiered tulle, makes one wish he knew the girls in the fading photo. Why does the one in the center look like she would rather be somewhere else? What's her story? Did she find happiness and marry after she caught the bride's bouquet? Was she also in love with the bride's groom? Or, did she lead a solitary life before she committed suicide? Perhaps she's contemplating poetry in the picture and she's not sad after all. Have we read her poems? Did she write about the time period when she posed for the photographer, after the Great Depression but before the Second World War? Or, did she write about what was in her heart and in her thoughts?

We take turns pawing through piles of snapshots and portraits, wishing the scavengers had left them in order inside their aging scrapbooks so we could give the elegant people a purpose, a place within the scheme of life, even if we couldn't provide names. And then, I saw her.

Not an image of my sister-in-law, but a photo of a girl who looks like her. The woman would now be forty years my relative's senior. The woman staring back at me from the black-and-white photo looks too mysterious for someone who could count only two decades of her life.

She's probably not related to my sister-in-law, but who knows for sure? I flip the photo over, holding my breath, hoping to see a name or a date. But, neither surfaces. Her half-smile haunts me when I look at the photo again. I must have her. No matter what the price, she goes home with me. She has no apparent connection to the wedding party, but the girls in it have also spoken to me. They deserve more than a crushed jumble inside a cardboard box. I wonder what will happen to all my pictures, those of my own kin and others like these that no one knows, when I die. I pay for my new treasures.

Am I now a scavenger also? Am I a collector that moves unknown printed people to a strange new place or am I one who rescues them, giving fragile persons new names, and adopts them into my family.

Adopt this easy-to-make cake and your family may want to give it a new name. Delicious, Outstanding or Awesome come to mind.

Wacky Chocolate Cake

3 cups flour
2 cups sugar
2 teaspoons baking soda
1 teaspoon salt
1/3 cup cocoa
2 cups water
2 tablespoons vinegar
¾ cup salad oil
1 teaspoon vanilla

Preheat oven to 350°.

Sift flour, sugar, soda and salt into mixing bowl. Combine water, vinegar, oil and vanilla in small bowl; add to dry ingredients and mix with a spoon.

Bake in an ungreased 13"x9" cake pan for 30 minutes. Remove from oven and let cool. Frost cake with powdered sugar icing.

Powdered Sugar Icing

1 (16-ounce) box powdered sugar
1 stick (½ cup) margarine
1 teaspoon vanilla
Small amount of whole milk

Cream margarine in bowl of electric mixer; beat in powdered sugar. Add vanilla and milk, a teaspoon at a time, and beat until icing is of spreading consistency; then, beat a little longer. Spread icing on cooled cake.

Turquoise

turquoise is a rock
polished, it becomes a gem
and graces a hand

Favorite gems in my kitchen form a long list, but Cherry Cheese Pie, Chocolate Sheath Cake and Cherry Crunch are requested often, by as many men as women. You can't go wrong with these desserts.

Cherry Cheese Pie

1 (8-ounce) package cream cheese, at room temperature
1 (14-ounce) can sweetened condensed milk
1/3 cup lemon juice
1 teaspoon vanilla
1 (9-inch) graham cracker pie crust
1 (21-ounce) can cherry pie filling

Beat cream cheese until fluffy in large mixing bowl; gradually add condensed milk; beating until smooth. Stir in lemon juice and vanilla; blend well. Pour mixture into pie crust. Chill in refrigerator about 3 hours. Remove pie from refrigerator and spread pie filling on top of cream cheese pie; return pie to refrigerator to chill until set. Slice and serve cold.

Seed Power

"She came from the seedy side of town," the novel reads. When did seedy adopt such a negative connotation? Seeds have never fallen from grace, so we gardeners can outlaw "seedy" and banish it from our vocabularies.

As natural as breathing, seeds demand a more positive place in our world. Without seeds, how would fruits, vegetables and trees reproduce? Birds would feel lost if denied the delicacy of seeds. Human sperm, like other living creatures, germinates from seeds as do ideas and patterns for our social and financial lives.

From seeds that fill the palm of your hand to those no larger than a dark speck, delicate and fragile, we are treated to exotic blooms, luscious fruit, and towering trees. The formation of new ideas, plans for success, the search for everlasting life, and hope for a nation all sprout from a single embryo. Our world revolves around seeds, whether visible in nature or transparent in emotion. To touch or imagine, seeds rule!

Find your seed. Plant it, nurture it and watch it grow. Enjoy its beauty and savor the experience. Then, find another and another and…

Where would be without seeds? Besides seed power in life, food production, and flower gardening, ideas germinate, businesses start from seed money, etc. We wouldn't want to give up sesame seeds to garnish hamburger buns and chicken wings, sunflower seeds to snack on, poppy seeds on muffins, and more.

Slow-Cooker Chicken Wings

3 pounds chicken wing pieces
2 tablespoons bacon grease or shortening
½ cup red wine vinegar
1½ cups ketchup
¼ cup packed dark brown sugar
1 tablespoon yellow mustard
2 tablespoons Worcestershire sauce
¼ teaspoon garlic powder
½ teaspoon salt
¼ teaspoon black pepper
2 tablespoons sesame seeds
Bleu cheese salad dressing
Ranch salad dressing
Barbecue sauce
Hot pepper sauce

Grease the inside of a 5-quart slow cooker.

Heat bacon grease in a large skillet and brown wing pieces, adding more grease if needed. Remove from heat and transfer chicken to prepared slow cooker.

In a bowl, combine vinegar, ketchup, sugar, mustard, Worcestershire sauce, garlic powder, salt, and pepper; mix well. Pour over wings in slow cooker; toss gently.

Cover slow cooker; cook 4 hours on low setting.

To serve, remove chicken wings from the slow cooker with a slotted spoon; pile wings on a serving platter. Sprinkle wings with sesame seeds.

Pour salad dressings and barbecue sauce into individual dipping bowls; set a bottle of hot sauce on the table. Serve wings while hot.

The Fork

Which way should I go?

When my life is in turmoil, I question everything. I'm unsure which fork in the road I should take. Which one is mine?

Does one lead to peace and happiness, and the other to more crisis? How can I know unless I take both? Follow one long enough to see where it leads me, then can I backtrack and take the other one?

Not so. Even if I could do that, it would not be a fair evaluation. For, you see, once I've traveled down the first path, I've changed. My life has been enriched with pleasure or attacked by negatives. I am not the same person who first weighed the pros and cons of going left or right.

There are no correct answers in life. We make choices many times a day, some small and a few that change the direction for the rest of our lives. We are who we are until we make decisions. Then, we are who we become. Although changed by choice or circumstance, from that point forward, we again are who we are. Life evolves and so do we.

What if the intersection looming ahead is no fork or "Y"? It is a four-way. I could retreat and go back the way I came, but who wants to go backward? That leaves me three choices to ponder. Which way should I go?

When you have difficult choices to make or questions to resolve, try baking bread. Unless you're a sculptor or a potter creating in clay, nothing removes stress quicker than kneading bread. Besides making something delicious to eat, and wonderful to smell while in the oven, the process of kneading and working the dough with your hands tends to relax your frayed nerves, slowing down a stressful day and giving you time to concentrate on the whys and what ifs. Good luck on making the right decisions in your life.

This is the recipe my mom always used for hot rolls. They were the best!

Mom's Hot Rolls

2 packages yeast (yeast cakes, if you can find them)
¼ cup lukewarm water
1 cup whole milk
½ cup sugar
1 teaspoon salt
¼ cup shortening
5 cups all-purpose flour
2 eggs
Butter, for glazing

Soften yeast in water; set aside. Scald milk in large saucepan; stir in sugar, salt and shortening; cool to lukewarm. Stir in 2 cups flour, or enough to make a thick batter. Add eggs and yeast mixture; beat well. Stir in more flour, enough to make a soft dough. Turn out on a lightly-floured board; knead until smooth and satiny with tiny gas bubbles under the surface. Place dough in a greased bowl; cover and let rise in a warm place for about an hour, or until doubled in size. Punch dough down; let stand 10 minutes; shape into rolls and place into greased pans. Let rise for about an hour or until doubled. Bake in a pre-heated oven at 350° for 20-30 minutes.

Glaze tops of hot rolls with butter. Yield: about 3½ dozen rolls.

This same recipe can be made into loaves.

Using the same Mom's Hot Rolls recipe, roll out the dough for Cinnamon Rolls; slather it with butter, sprinkle with cinnamon and sugar, slice; and let rise in pans. Baking time remains the same. Mom made these often.

Another good recipe came from one of her sisters.

Aunt Lucy's Cinnamon Rolls

2 packages yeast
2 tablespoons sugar
1 cup lukewarm water
¾ cup sugar
½ cup margarine
1 cup warm milk
1 tablespoon salt
3 eggs, beaten
7 cups flour
Additional margarine and sugar
Raisins
Nuts
Cinnamon
Powdered sugar and milk for glaze

In small bowl, dissolve yeast and 2 tablespoons sugar in water. Set aside.

In a large bowl, mix ¾ cup sugar, margarine, milk, salt, and eggs. Add 2 cups flour; mix well. Add yeast mixture; stir until combined. Add remaining 5 cups flour; mix well. Knead mixture lightly into a ball. Let rise until doubled. Punch down and roll out to ½ inch.

Spread lots of melted butter and sprinkle with cinnamon, sugar, raisins, and nuts. Roll dough into a long and slice in ½ pieces. Place into a greased tin. Let rise again.

Bake at 375° for 20-25 minutes.

Glaze rolls while hot.

Stress

Evening's calm repose
chases away life's struggles.
Demons wake at dawn.

Don't stress out over the small things; life offers enough crises for us to exercise our coping skills. Get in the kitchen and experiment. Baking is an excellent antidote to stress. No time? Throw something in a bread-making machine, pour yourself a cup of soothing hot tea, and let the aroma of fresh bread calm you.

Hawaiian Sweet Bread

2/3 cup pineapple juice
1 egg white
3 tablespoons milk
1 teaspoon vanilla
1/3 teaspoon salt
¼ cup granulated sugar
2½ cups bread flour
1/3 cup potato flakes
1 teaspoon quick-rising yeast
2½ tablespoons butter

Pour pineapple juice, egg white, milk and vanilla into pan of electric bread maker. Add salt, sugar, flour and potato flakes. Make a well in the center and add dry yeast. Cut butter into small pieces and place in each of the four corners of the bread maker pan. Bake at Regular bread setting for 3 hours and 10 minutes. Remove from pan and let cool. Slice and serve.

Once a Cowgirl

Olivia definitely had the gift of gaud, that's G-A-U-D. Multiple strands of Mardi-Gras necklaces rested on her ample bosom and fake gold coins hung from her pendulous earlobes. She wore a simple housedress and had three feather boas intertwined with long red scarves around her short neck. Her ebony skin once shined like satin before it aged to a dull ash and weathered like elephant hide.

The bar's smoky haze hid its few afternoon patrons. Olivia crept inside to enjoy air conditioning before the happy hour crowd rushed in after a day's work. She removed her scarves and boas, rolling them around her hand and elbow like she used to reel a rope. How long had it been since she'd worked horses? Leaving the ranch years ago still pained her, but she didn't dwell on the past. Nearly everyone she knew lost their horses, cattle and sprawling ranch homes in the eighties. When the oil boom went bust in Oklahoma, most of the banks closed their doors and the lucrative jobs dried up. People couldn't pay their bills or house payments, so the mortgage companies stepped in. Only the foreclosure attorneys made money that decade.

Olivia never recovered her home. She sold all five of her palomino beauties and cried when the semi hauled those faithful four-legged friends to a buyer in Montana. A deep sigh escaped Olivia's parched lips.

"At least, they have plenty to eat again and lots of room to run," she mumbled and arranged her assortment of canvas and plastic bags beside her ankle.

The bartender glided over to Olivia's small table in the corner. He slipped her a glass of wine while she sat almost hidden in the shadows.

She smiled her thanks for the treat.

"Hurry," he said. "The boss went upstairs to do the deposit. You need to be out of here before he comes back down."

"I will," she said. Sipping the garnet liquid, Olivia fingered her garish necklaces, lost in thought. She heard footsteps but failed to differentiate between the soft retreat of her experienced server and the rapid approach of the bar's angry proprietor.

"Shoo!" the owner shouted. "Get out of here, you old witch."

Refusing to make a scene, Olivia left the bar but struck a regal pose for her exit. She admitted her homeless state and her poor wardrobe choices, but she still counted as a good woman. She talked to herself while she walked on broken sidewalks bordering streets of red brick older than her years.

"Son-of-a-gun, anyway." She sniffed and rubbed the end of her nose, willing herself not to cry. Instead, she camouflaged her feelings by letting her mind race; she was astride Mandolay. "For a few minutes, that yellow gelding and I can fly across a sea of prairie grass again." Olivia stopped for a red traffic light to turn green, but continued to talk, ignoring stares from motorists.

A shiny green Dodge truck with matching horse trailer whizzed by, running the caution light. Loaded with four paint horses, only the truck made it through the intersection before the light turned red.

"Somebody's in an awful hurry." Olivia pointed at the disappearing rig. "Be careful with those valuable horses, you fool. Did you forget you had a trailer following you?" She let her mind wander as she walked to a rougher part of town, her home for the last ten or twelve years – she couldn't remember exactly. She hoped no one had confiscated her cardboard box while she strolled the downtown streets. Exercise had kept her healthy and memorizing street names kept her reading and spelling skills intact. She knew every one-way street and detour in downtown Oklahoma City and gave excellent directions when travelers plied her with questions and bewildered looks on their faces. She stopped and, with both hands on her hips, bragged, "I'm a walking gazetteer."

Olivia waved at the pastor when she walked by one of many small churches within a mile-radius of downtown. She would visit with him again when the temperature dipped below ten degrees. Only then, would she sleep in the shelter run by the church. The rest of the time, she let others who were less fortunate than she partake of the community spirit donated by rich people from elite neighborhoods, those few who hadn't lost everything when the oil boom faded or who moved into the state after the bust and picked up bargains when real estate hit an all-time low.

"There he goes again," Olivia said, when the green truck and horse trailer flew by, going the wrong way on a one-way street. "I hope you get straightened out soon. Stop and water those horses in this July heat," she yelled.

Seeing the paints reminded Olivia of her first love. "Oh, Marvin, I wonder what ever happened to you." She sat down on a bench, but waved the bus on by when it slowed. "I'll never forget that last day, before you left for college. In Texas, wasn't it? You rode your mare Ginger, the prettiest markings on a paint ever, and I rode behind you, my arms holding you so tight you asked me to stop so you could breathe. I didn't want to let you go, afraid I would never see you again. Boy, did I have reason to be afraid." She smoothed her wind-blown hair. "We had a wonderful picnic lunch that afternoon. I can almost taste that fried chicken today."

Her stomach growled, just thinking about food. She shaded her eyes with her hand to look toward the sun, an orange ball settling into the horizon. She recognized a sales clerk from the local thrift shop coming her way. "Hi, Martha. Got your day in?"

"You bet, Olivia." Martha sat beside the gaudy-attired woman. "There's one more truck coming in with donations, but I couldn't wait. I have to catch my bus or I can't get home tonight."

"This is the last one to your part of town, Martha. You shouldn't have to work overtime unless you want to, anyway." Olivia perked up. "How about if I go meet the truck? I can help unload and package the stuff. I've seen you guys do it a hundred times."

"No," said Martha, "they wouldn't let you."

"But," Olivia said before slowing her enthusiasm and sitting on a park-style bench. "Of course, they won't. Homeless. I forgot for a minute."

Martha fidgeted before saying, "I'm sorry."

Olivia waved the apology away. "No problem. It's just life." She removed her feather boas and stuffed them into one of the many plastic bags she carried.

"I don't mean to be nosey, Olivia, but why do you wear those things? Especially in this heat. Aren't you miserable?"

"Sure, I'm hot," Olivia answered. "But, they keep my neck and shoulders from burning. You know how fast that sun can cook you."

"Yeah, makes sense."

Martha looked like she needed to apologize. "But, I wish you'd find something nice to wear. Just for a change, you know."

"I know, Martha. May I'll saunter over and see what's new tomorrow."

"That'd be great," Martha said. "Here's my chariot. Gotta go." She ran up the steps of the city bus, turned and waved.

Olivia stood up, gathered up her bags, and headed toward a small wooded area, the place she called home.

That night, barrel-racing dominated Olivia's dreams. Seeing the horse heads poking out of their trailer earlier in the day must have triggered a response. As a young woman, Olivia wrapped herself in the warm glow of the rodeo circuit, a close-knit family with a competitive spirit. She made enough money to race around 50-gallon drums instead of getting a steady job. Then, she bought her own livestock and, when oil became King, she went in debt for her own ranch, including ranch hands.

She enjoyed that dream for a couple of years until the fantasy dried up and turned as black as the oil that once sprang from her pasture. She thought about rodeoing again but couldn't justify begging someone to haul her around and provide everything for her. Most of her rodeo family mirrored her dilemma, some losing new mansions they'd built before their oil fortunes went belly up. Remembering several of her neighbor's suicides made her wince.

Bright sunlight pierced its way through a canopy of leaves to announce daylight to a cluster of homeless souls. Olivia squeezed her eyes shut for a moment to let her eyes adjust to another hot summer day, then washed up in a nearby creek before starting her morning rounds. She picked up more hubcaps and aluminum cans that morning than she ever had before. Once in front of the thrift shop, she sucked in her breath and clasped her hands in front of her in prayer fashion. She couldn't believe her eyes. The mannequin in the window wore a cowgirl's rodeo outfit similar to the ones Olivia once wore. Olivia rushed inside and located Martha. They stripped the mannequin so Olivia could try on the clothes. Both women wore astonished looks on their faces. The clothes fit! Willing to get down on her knees, Olivia begged the young woman not to sell the cowgirl's suit.

"I can hold it for you, Olivia, but only until tomorrow," Martha said.

"I'll be back for it. I promise," Olivia said and changed back into her day dress.

After selling her cans and hubcaps, Olivia stuffed the money into her cleavage. When she reached her makeshift home, it was high noon. Everyone else was gone, either to look for work or to the mission for lunch. She unpinned a small cosmetic bag from her underwear and counted her stash. Adding the morning's cash, the homeless woman had enough money to buy the donated cowgirl suit.

Olivia smiled and whistled a tune while rushing to the thrift store. She paid Martha for the suit and had a few quarters left. Olivia put the change inside the front pants pocket and told Martha, "This is the first time I've had a pocket in a long time."

Martha's boss had gone to lunch so Martha hustled Olivia into the back of the store to let her clean up properly before donning the almost-new suit. Olivia expressed her thanks and left the store, her attitude changed forever. She felt transformed, like a real person again, one that could maybe not conquer the world but meet it head on. She decided to use one of her quarters to call a former neighbor that somehow managed to keep his ranch together and ask him for a job. She'd muck out stalls just for room and board if he'd let her. If not, maybe he knew someone who would.

Crossing the street to a pay phone, Olivia had to hurry to keep from getting run over by the same green Dodge pickup and horse trailer that she had seen the day before. But this time, the rig traveled a little slower and pulled over to a stop a short ways from her. Olivia walked down there to offer travel directions.

The driver pushed a button to roll down the truck's window on the passenger side and smiled at Olivia. He gave her a soft wolf whistle and said, "Mighty fine." Then, he asked, "Rodeo girl?"

"Used to run the barrels," Olivia answered. "Looks like you're lost. Maybe I can help." She decided this man must not have been out in the sun much; his skin was so smooth and almost as dark and shiny as his eyes. He reminded her of Marvin and she gave her head a little shake to keep from daydreaming before asking, "Where you headed?"

"I'm on my way to a horse sale in Montana and thought I'd catch the rodeo in Cheyenne on the way. Want to come?"

Olivia pondered his question for a few seconds before she reached for the door handle.

Author's Note: Although my Olivia and her circumstances are fictional, she sometimes interrupts my day to tell me there is more to her story – enough for a novel or novella. Look for "The Search for Mandolay" in the future.

Cowboy Stew

1½ pounds ground beef
1 onion, chopped
5 potatoes, cooked until almost tender
1 large can ranch-style beans
1 can tomato soup
1 can chopped tomatoes
1 small can mild chili peppers
1 hot chili pepper (optional)
1 can whole kernel corn
Salt
Black pepper

In a soup pot, brown ground beef and onion; drain grease. Add potatoes, beans with juice, soup, tomatoes, chili peppers, and corn; stir well. Cover and simmer 1 hour. Add salt and pepper, to taste.
Serve warm.

The Silent War

Will we ever know peace again? I mulled that thought over for the umpteenth time this afternoon.

Blake shifted in his seat beside me. Although we sat in tufted theater seats, he looked as uncomfortable as the guy who squirms in his chair in the hemorrhoid commercial. I glanced at my husband from the corner of my eye. Serves him right. He shouldn't have poo-pooed the warnings. I touched his shoulder.

"Sorry, Robin," he whispered.

I smiled my acceptance of his apology, wondering whether it was for his wiggling or if it was regret for a bigger transgression. We should have built an air-tight shelter before now. It could have protected us from Oklahoma tornadoes in peacetime and now this. We transferred our attention back to the government official at the podium who continued his litany in a matter-of-fact voice.

"Listen for 21 bells from the bell tower. We chose 21, to mirror the 21-gun salute, to honor any who may have perished. When those bells of freedom ring," he advised, "they will be the signal to resume our daily lives. Until then, we should cower, yes cower, in storm shelters, drink bottled water, and eat dried and pre-packaged foods that we stashed in earlier months."

"That won't be us," Blake whispered, his dark eyes full of concern.

I guess the official had rehearsed his speech and delivered it in almost every major city in our troubled country. After hearing himself drone on, repeating the same phrases, he was probably numb to most of its content.

"There were bomb shelters and air raid sirens in the two world wars," he said. "No need for that now. The new enemy is the air we breathe – weapons of mass destruction designed to travel on air currents and infiltrate tiny nooks and crannies until we inhale it through our nostrils and allow it to poison our lungs. It enters the pores of our flesh and attacks our nervous system, turns our muscles into liquid pockets, and imprisons our blood cells in mesh cages." He waited for the desired impact.

The audience struggled with the graphic news and reacted with cries of alarm, weeping, and emotional hugs. Not one person questioned the validity of his message.

The official waited for the premature grief and murmurs to die down, then lashed out with the next volley. "The danger is here! Those who have no storm shelters will be the first wave of victims."

"Now, he's talking about us," I said, but I forgot to whisper. No one looked my way, like people do when someone speaks out during a movie, so I must have voiced the same fear that most of them were dealing with. I snuggled into Blake's side, thinking how we would all be homeless inside our own houses.

"Only those who plan ahead stand a chance for endurance and victory over such a vile and invisible enemy," the official stated. "Few will survive to populate the new world. But, what will they see when they emerge from their shelters? Imagine the nation's ground, littered with rotting corpses of humans and animals."

"With television documenting every battle," Blake whispered, "we said the Gulf War was fought in our living rooms. This one will rage in our own front yards."

Two men raised their hands to speak.

"Who will do the cleanup? Isn't that the government's job?"

"How long will it take to dispose of the remains?"

"It could take months to bury the dead," the official answered. "Too monumental a task for the few who are left. Gas masks are still rationed, and we don't know how effective they will be with long-term usage." He cleared his throat and mopped his brow. "Setting fire to acres and acres of cadaver-strewn land sounds like the best plan," he said "but the acrid stench would overpower the hardiest of warriors. And, would they not be exposed again to the poisons in the air, carried by huge plumes of smoke? Charcoal clouds, silent carriers of doom, can spiral into eternity."

"And hopefully," I added, "into nothingness." I nudged Blake. "Perhaps they will be the silence before the next peace."

He nodded. "I hope we can get the rest of the materials to finish our shelter in time."

We gathered up our coats and walked out into the sunshine.

No parking places opened up at Lowe's so we drove to Home Depot. Blake let me out of the pickup so he could pull into a sliver of a parking space. When we entered the home center, we looked back outside to see if the sun still shone. We experienced the same pandemonium from the crowd inside that we had learned to expect in winter from pending snow and ice storms. Long lines at checkout registers, frantic shoppers and clerks, and gaping holes greeted us where merchandise had been snatched from shelves. We shoved through a break in the traffic to get dry cement, vent hoses, locks, and door hinges.

"Grab these cases of bottled water," I said and did a spread-eagle stretch with my arms and torso to keep a couple of guys away until Blake could load the precious liquid on our cart. Blake doesn't show stress often, but he looked worried.

"We'd better go," he said.

We shoved the heavy cart to checkout, and he headed outside. He had the pickup parked at the door by the time I paid for our purchases. We drove to the grocery store.

Long lines of frightened customers outside Homeland and Wal-Mart confirmed our fears. Panic had already set in, and food would be nonexistent by the time we could enter either store. Neither one of us spoke, but I'm pretty sure we both knew that we'd have to survive on what food and supplies we had at home. I wanted to joke that he was fortunate to have a wife who was a packrat, but we both remained silent.

Neighbors who hadn't gone to the briefing met us when we pulled into our driveway.

"How bad is it?" They wanted to know, and we needed to share the devastating news, but I clammed up. I could not be the voice of doom. Blake, my strong, silent- type guy, repeated the presentation verbatim.

Appalled that he could remember, or even hear that much, I laid into him. "You do have selective hearing! You can hear and you can process information – when you choose to." Our neighbors laughed at him. Their actions tempered my anger, but only a little. What they offered up then changed my mad to glad.

Living side-by-side in houses across the street from us, they invited us to move in with them until this pending danger was over.

"Or until the end of the world, whichever comes first," Joe's wife, Roxanne, said. "Joe and Harvey here not only built an underground shelter – they built a Man Cave that connects both houses."

"That's right," Harvey said. "We wanted to protect ourselves from terrorists, if we could, but not let that space and all our hard work go to waste."

"Yeah," Joe said. "We're anxious for football season to start, and we'll be in our Man Cave until it ends." Their laughter brightened my spirits.

"Really," Roxanne said. "It is huge. Plenty big enough for three couples. They've wired it and plumbed it – everything we need to eat, bathe, and sleep in our houses is duplicated in their Man Cave. Bring over all the food, water, and necessities you have. We'll tough it out as long as we need to."

Blake and I looked at each other, then at our gracious neighbors. "Are you absolutely sure?" We asked that in unison.

"You bet," the three of them chorused.

"Beverly is holding down the fort," Roxanne said. "We'll let her know you're coming. None of us have forgotten how you took care of her while Harvey served in Iraq and Afghanistan."

Blake shrugged his shoulders and said, "Aw, we didn't do anything."

"Not what I heard," Harvey said. He and Joe shook Blake's hand and hugged me.

"Blake fixed her car and maintained their yard," Joe said, "but he wasn't the one who cooked and cleaned for Beverly when she got sick and endured months of treatment."

"Just being neighborly," I said.

The three of them crossed the street to advise Beverly there would be six for dinner tonight. Blake and I unloaded the pickup and started planning the evacuation from our home.

"When this is all over, and I hope it passes over," Blake said, "I *will* finish our shelter and stock it just in case we run into this nightmare again. I really will."

"Living with four other adults," I said, "for who knows how long may not be easy, you know. Even good people like these."

"Yeah," my husband said, "but it's our best chance to keep on living."

The Silent War is a piece of fiction, but there are times we need to have food with a long shelf life on hand. Homemade jerky is a favorite of many and is usually devoured long before it ages. With tornadoes, floods, hurricanes, snowstorms, and other disasters, jerky, dried fruit, nuts, bottled water, etc. should be staples in our homes. These items work well for long car trips and camping, too.

Beef Jerky

1½ -2 pounds flank steak
2/3 cup Worcestershire sauce
2/3 cup soy sauce
1 tablespoon honey
2 teaspoons freshly-ground black pepper
2 teaspoons onion powder
1 teaspoon liquid smoke
1 teaspoon red pepper flakes

Trim the steak of any excess fat; discard fat. Place meat strips in a zip-top plastic bag, and place it in the freezer for 1-2 hours in order to firm up. Remove steak from the freezer and thinly slice the meat, with the grain, into long strips.

Place the strips of meat and all of the remaining ingredients into a 1-gallon plastic zip-top bag, moving meat around to evenly distribute all of the ingredients. Place the bag into the refrigerator for 3-6 hours.

Remove the meat from the brine and pat dry. Evenly distribute the strips of meat onto dehydrator trays. Allow the meat to dry, following the manufacturer's directions.

Once dry, store in an airtight container in a cool, dry place for 2-3 months.

Legacy

Suddenly, I felt a hole in my heart.
I felt it so deep – this hole in my heart,
should have guessed his destiny from the start.

He was a young rebel, yet fair and kind.
He pushed the limits – this rebellious kind.
Oh, how he almost made me lose my mind.

We saw the arc when he became a dad,
witnessing what changed him – this single dad –
the most important role he'd ever had.

Who knew my son would leave this earth so soon?
Yes, my son flew to heaven far too soon,
honored by those who thought he'd hung the moon.

Weeping, I serve his young children ice cream,
wishing we could wake from this cruel dream.

(Poetry Form: Blues Sonnet)

Monte Shepherd championed the underdog and always helped others, especially when they were in crisis. He was funny, bright, hard-working, caring, and blessed with friendships. When he was thirty-seven, he requested I write a cookbook so he would have proven recipes to cook for his young children, but his sudden passing came before the book was finished.

Chess Pie is one of the recipes my son Monte wanted in the cookbook. When he started school in California long ago, he completed his work in kindergarten and first grade so early that he was bored and began to cause trouble in his classroom. School administrators suggested he be tested. I took him for a battery of tests, and the results showed no problems. However, with an IQ of 143, the professionals said he needed a challenge so he learned to play chess in first grade. The school allowed him to compete that year in chess tournaments against sixth-graders! After he won several matches, he somehow heard about Chess Pie. I found a recipe, made the pie, and he asked for it often.

Southern Chess Pie

4 eggs
½ cup butter
1½ cups sugar
2 tablespoons evaporated milk
2 tablespoons yellow cornmeal
1/8 teaspoon salt
2 tablespoons lemon juice
2 teaspoons vanilla
Pastry for 9-inch pie

Preheat oven to 325°. Combine eggs, butter and sugar in mixing bowl. Beat 5 minutes at high speed on mixer. Blend in milk, cornmeal, salt, lemon juice and vanilla. Pour mixture into pastry-lined pie pan. Bake 55-60 minutes or until set and crust is browned. Let cool.

Almost Well

I've cheated death again, God
I'm told there must be more for me to do here on earth

Whatever that may be I have no clue
Others tell me it must be huge
because death has been shoved aside several times

I hope I'm up to the challenge
You'll have to guide me for sure

Reveal Your plan for me when the time is right
I am Yours

Author's note: Since I wrote this poem, I faced death again. It's a little frightening when the doctors give up on you again and also when it's the third time. The third time's the charm, as they say, and I thought I might get it (death) right. But, I'm still here, praying that God uses me as He sees fit.

I hope you enjoy making the recipes in this book. They are a sampling of the many (zillions?) I've accumulated.

Happy cooking to you!

More favorite family recipes

Appetizers

QUICK 'N EASY SALMON PATTIES (Serves 4-6)

1 can (15-16 ounces) pink salmon
1 egg
1/3 cup minced onion

1/2 cup flour
1 1/2 teaspoons baking powder
1-1/2 cups Crisco

Drain salmon, set aside 2 tablespoons of the juice. In a medium mixing bowl, mix salmon, egg and onion until sticky. Stir in flour. Add baking powder to salmon juice; stir into salmon mixture. Form into small patties and fry until golden brown (about 5 minutes) in hot Crisco. Serve with tartar sauce or Caesar salad dressing.

Fruit Dip

1 cup sour cream
4 tablespoons apricot preserves
3 tablespoons pecans or walnuts, chopped fine
½ cup fresh coconut, grated
1½ teaspoons orange rind, minced

Fruit for dipping:
Sliced bananas, whole strawberries, apple chunks, grapes, and Mandarin oranges.

Mix sour cream, apricot preserves, nuts, coconut and orange rind in small bowl or food processor. Transfer mixture to a small serving bowl; cover and place in refrigerator to chill. Serve cold dip in center of platter, surrounded by fruit.

Pineapple Cheese Balls

2 (8-ounce) packages cream cheese, softened
1 (8 ½-ounce) can crushed pineapple, drained well
¼ cup green pepper, chopped fine
2 tablespoons onion, minced
1 tablespoon seasoned salt
2 cups pecans, chopped

Beat cream cheese until smooth. Add pineapple, green pepper, onion, seasoned salt and 1 cup pecans; blend. Form 2 large balls and roll each in ½ cup pecans. Cover with plastic wrap; then with foil. Chill.

Easy Cheese Balls

2 (8-ounce) packages cream cheese
1½ ounces cheddar cheese, grated
1 envelope Hidden Valley® Ranch Dressing, original flavor
Chopped pecans

Allow cream cheese and cheddar cheese to come to room temperature. in a mixing bowl, blend cheeses until smooth. Add powdered dressing gradually until all of it is combined. Wrap in mixture in plastic wrap and refrigerate for an hour or so.

Remove mixture from refrigerator; shape into balls and roll in enough pecans to coat. Wrap cheese balls in fresh plastic wrap; chill until serving time.

Yield: 2 cheese balls or 1 large one.

Redneck Caviar Dip

2 (16-ounce) cans black-eyed peas, drained
1 (16-ounce) can white or yellow hominy, drained
3 green onions, chopped
1¼ cups white onions, chopped
2 jalapeno peppers, chopped fine
2 tomatoes, chopped
1 cup parsley, chopped
1 garlic clove, minced
1 (8-ounce) bottle Italian salad dressing
Tortilla chips or large corn chips

In a mixing bowl, combine first 8 ingredients; mix well. Add dressing; toss to incorporate. Cover and chill at least 2 hours before serving.

To serve, spoon dip mixture into serving bowl. Place bowl of chips nearby.

Chili con Queso

1 can diced tomatoes
1 can diced tomatoes with green chilies
1 small onion, diced
2 garlic cloves, minced
1 teaspoon vegetable or olive oil
1 (8-ounce) package cream cheese, cut into cubes
6 ounces Velveeta, cut into cubes
1 teaspoon chili powder
2 tablespoons minced cilantro
Tortilla chips

Pour both cans tomatoes into colander; drain, reserving 1/3 cup liquid; set aside. Discard remaining liquid.

In a large skillet, saute onion and garlic in oil until tender but not brown. Add cream cheese; stir until melted. Reduce heat to low; stir in Velveeta, chili powder, tomatoes, and reserved liquid; cook until cheese is melted. Remove from heat. Stir in cilantro.

Keep queso dip warm in a chafing dish, fondue pot, or small slow cooker. Serve beside a bowl of tortilla chips.

Hamburger Cheese Dip

1 pound hamburger meat, browned, drained, and crumbled
3 cans Frito Lay® Jalapeno Cheese Dip
3 cans Frito Lay® Mild Cheddar Dip
1 cup milk
1 can cream of mushroom soup

Mix all ingredients together in a slow cooker; heat on low setting for 30-40 minutes, stirring occasionally.

Dip is ready to serve when heated through.

Keep warm for serving.

Leftover dip should be kept, covered, in the refrigerator and may be reheated.

Note: Adjust ratio of jalapeno cheese dip to mild cheddar dip for a milder or hotter dip.

The recipe may be doubled in a large slow cooker.

Salsa

4 large tomatoes, peeled and chopped
1 medium onion, peeled and chopped
1 large green bell pepper, seeded and chopped
1 jalapeno pepper,
1 serrano pepper
1 garlic clove
1 tablespoon sugar
2½ teaspoons salt
¾ teaspoon cumin
2 tablespoons fresh lemon juice
1 (6-ounce) can tomato paste
¼ cup cider apple vinegar
Chips

Peel and chop tomatoes and onion. Seed and chop the peppers. Peel and mince garlic.

In a large saucepan, combine all ingredients except chips; stir and bring slowly to a boil. Reduce heat; simmer for 1 hour, uncovered; stir often. Remove from heat; let cool.

When salsa comes to room temperature, cover and refrigerate.

Serve chilled with tortilla chips, thick corn chips, or sturdy snack crackers.

Guacamole

2 ripe avocados
½ cup yogurt
½ cup sour cream
1 small onion
2 plum tomatoes
1-2 jalapeno peppers
1 tablespoon minced cilantro
½ teaspoon salt
2 tablespoons fresh lime juice
Chips

Peel and pit avocados. Strain yogurt, blotting with paper towel to dry as much as possible. In a mixing bowl, combine one avocado, yogurt, and sour cream; beat until blended.

Peel and chop onion. Peel and seed tomatoes and pepper. Add onion, tomatoes, pepper, cilantro, and salt, to yogurt mixture; stir.

Mash second avocado with lime juice in a small bowl; add to guacamole mixture; stir to combine. Serve immediately.

Quick Guacamole Dip

1 cup mashed avocado
¼ cup finely-chopped onion
¼ cup mayonnaise
½ teaspoon salt
1 teaspoon lemon juice
2 tablespoons green chilies
1 small tomato, peeled and seeded
Raw vegetables or chips

Combine all ingredients in a small bowl; mix well. Cover and chill for 1 hour.

Serve with sliced raw vegetables or corn chips.

Note: Picante sauce may be substituted, if desired, for the lemon juice, green chilies, and tomato for an even quicker dip.

Hot Ham Dip

4 ounces Swiss cheese
2/3 cup mayonnaise
1 (8-ounce) package cream cheese, softened
1 tablespoon brown mustard
1 tablespoon finely-chopped green bell pepper
1½ cups diced cooked ham
2 tablespoons butter, melted
¾ cup rye cracker crumbs
Thin slices green bell pepper, for garnish
Tortilla chips or sturdy crackers

Heat oven to 400°.
Have on hand a 9-inch pie plate with flared sides.
Shred cheese; set aside.
Combine mayonnaise and cream cheese in a small bowl; beat until smooth. Add shredded cheese, mustard, bell pepper, and ham; stir just to blend. Pour into an ungreased pie plate and spread in an even layer.

Mix butter with cracker crumbs; spread over ham mixture, leaving center almost bare of crumbs.

Bake, uncovered, for 12-15 minutes to heat through. Remove from oven.

Garnish center of dish with bell pepper slices. Serve warm with chips or crackers.

Baked Water Chestnuts

2 (8-ounce) cans whole water chestnuts, drained
1 cup soy sauce
1 cup granulated sugar
1 pound thinly-sliced bacon
(toothpicks)

In a small bowl, combine water chestnuts and soy sauce. Cover bowl and marinate in refrigerator for a minimum of 4 hours.

Remove bowl from refrigerator; drain liquid. Pour sugar into a pie plate; roll damp water chestnuts in sugar.

Preheat oven to 350°.

Lightly-grease a cookie sheet; set aside.

Wrap each water chestnut in a bacon strip, securing with a toothpick. (Cut bacon in short pieces, as needed, to have enough to wrap all water chestnuts.)

Place on prepared pan and bake until bacon is cooked through.

Serve warm.

Depression Meatballs

1½ pounds ground beef
2 eggs
½ cup grated cheese (parmesan or pecorino)
4 tablespoons finely-chopped onion
1 tablespoon dried parsley
½ cup bread crumbs
1 teaspoon salt
1 teaspoon black pepper
3 potatoes, boiled until tender
Vegetable or olive oil, for frying

In a large bowl, mash potatoes with a fork; let cool.

Add ground beef, eggs, cheese, onion, parsley, bread crumbs, salt, and pepper. Mix thoroughly. Form mixture into 1-inch balls; press balls into patties.

Heat oil in a skillet, fry meatball patties, in several batches, until browned and cooked through.

Drain on paper towels.

Serve warm.

Bacon Sticks

Wooden skewers
1 pound thick-sliced bacon
1 tablespoon vegetable shortening
1 cup semi-sweet chocolate chips
Chopped pecans
Toasted coconut

Put wooden skewers to soak in water for a few minutes.
Preheat oven to 400°.
Have ready a rimmed cookie sheet, lined with parchment paper.
Have ready a similar sheet; line it with waxed paper.
Thread each bacon strip onto a skewer, letting bacon ruffle. Place skewers on prepared pan. Do not crowd; use more than one parchment-lined pan, if needed. Bake 20-25 minutes or until crisp. Remove sheet pan from oven and bacon skewers from pan; cool bacon completely on a wire rack.

In a double-boiler, melt shortening and chocolate chips; stir until smooth. Remove from heat. Using a pastry brush, coat bacon on both sides with chocolate. Place on waxed-paper. Sprinkle with pecans or toasted coconut. Refrigerate until firm.

Store in refrigerator until ready to serve.

Variation: **White Bacon Sticks**
Follow directions above, except omit shortening and substitute white chocolate chips for the semi-sweet chocolate. Dice dried fruit (apricots, cherries or cranberries); sprinkle on bacon strips. Sprinkle some with chopped cashews.

Note: A microwave may be used in place of a double-boiler.

Polynesian Meat Medley

1 pound ground beef
1 egg
¼ cup dry bread crumbs
2 tablespoons milk
1 teaspoon salt
1/8 teaspoon ground nutmeg
½ pound chicken livers
2 tablespoons margarine
½ pound cocktail frankfurters
1 (14-ounce) can pineapple chunks (+ water, if needed)
¼ cup light brown sugar
2 tablespoons cornstarch
1 teaspoon chicken bouillon granules
3 tablespoons apple cider vinegar
1 tablespoon soy sauce

Preheat oven to 325°.

Combine ground beef, egg, bread crumbs, milk, salt and nutmeg in medium-sized mixing bowl; mix well. Form into ¾-inch balls. Set aside. Sauté chicken livers in margarine in large frying pan for 5 minutes or until they lose their pink color. Remove with slotted spoon and mound in 12-cup baking dish. Brown frankfurters in drippings in same pan; place in baking dish.

Sauté meatballs until well-browned in same pan; add to baking dish. Drain syrup from pineapple into a 1-cup measure; add water to make ¾ cup; set aside. Add drained pineapple to baking dish.

Mix brown sugar, cornstarch and chicken broth in small saucepan; stir in pineapple-juice mixture, vinegar and soy sauce. Cook, stirring constantly, until sauce thickens and boils 3 minutes. Pour over meats and pineapple in baking dish. Cover baking dish and bake for 30 minutes to blend flavors. Serve warm.

For parties, spoon mixture into a chafing dish.

Holiday Cheese Ring

4 cups shredded sharp cheddar cheese
1 cup finely-chopped pecans
1 cup mayonnaise
1 small onion, finely chopped
Pinch black pepper
Pinch cayenne pepper
Dash Worcestershire sauce
1 jar raspberry or strawberry preserves
Crackers

Grease a gelatin ring mold; set aside.

In a mixing bowl, blend together cheese, pecans, mayonnaise, onion, black and cayenne peppers, and Worcestershire sauce.

Spoon mixture evenly into ring mold. Place in refrigerator to chill 3-4 hours.

When chilled, transfer cheese ring from mold to serving plate. Spoon preserves into center of ring.

Serve with festive crackers.

Tropical Party Mix

2½ cups rice chex cereal
2½ cups corn chex cereal
1½ cup cashew nuts
½ cup macadamia nuts
¼ cup butter
2 tablespoons granulated sugar
2 tablespoons white corn syrup
¾ cup flaked coconut
1 cup white chocolate chips
4 ounces dried apricots
4 ounces dried pineapple

Place cereal and nuts in a large, microwave-safe bowl; set aside.

Cut butter into small cubes; combine it with sugar and syrup in a small, microwave-safe bowl. Microwave on high, uncovered, for 1 minute; stir; microwave 1 minute more; remove carefully from oven.

Pour mixture over cereal and nuts; transfer large bowl to microwave. Cook on high, uncovered, for 1 minute; stir; microwave 1 minute more; remove bowl from oven. Add coconut; return bowl to oven and microwave on high 1 minute; stir; cook 1 minute more; remove bowl from oven.

Spread mixture on parchment or waxed paper; let cool.

Chop apricots in half or in fourths if fruit is large. Chop pineapple to mirror size of apricot pieces.

Top cereal mixture with white chocolate chips, apricots, and pineapple. Stir gently to combine.

Serve immediately.

Store leftover party mix in an airtight container.

Chex Mix

3 cups corn chex cereal
3 cups rice chex cereal
3 cups wheat chex cereal
1 cup mixed nuts
1 cup pretzel twists
1 cup bite-size bagel chips
6 tablespoons butter
2 tablespoons Worcestershire sauce
1½ teaspoons seasoned salt
¾ teaspoon garlic powder

On kitchen counter, have ready a space covered with several layers of newspaper pages with paper towels on top.

In a large microwavable bowl, mix cereals, nuts, pretzel twists, and bagel chips; set aside. In small microwavable bowl, microwave butter on high setting, uncovered, for 40 seconds or until melted. Stir in seasonings. Pour over cereal mixture; stir until coated well; then microwave on high, uncovered, 5-6 minutes, stirring every 2 minutes. Remove from microwave; spread chex mixture on paper towels to cool.

Store in an airtight container.

Barbara's Chex Mix

4 cups corn chex cereal
3 cups rice chex cereal
1½ cups salted Virginia peanuts
1 cup salted cashew halves
2 cups tiny pretzel sticks
1 cup Cheerios®
1 stick + 1 tablespoon (9 tablespoons total) butter
2 tablespoons Worcestershire sauce
1½ teaspoons seasoned salt

Heat oven to 250°.

On kitchen counter, have ready a space covered with several layers of newspaper pages with paper towels on top.

In a large bowl, mix corn and rice cereals; set aside.

Melt even amounts of butter in two 13x9-inch baking pans; stir in Worcestershire sauce and seasoned salt. Add cereal mix to both pans; stir lightly to coat.

Bake 15 minutes; stir. Add nuts to both pans. Bake 15 more minutes. Add pretzel sticks and Cheerios® to both pans; stir to coat. Bake 30 minutes, stirring once.

Remove pans from oven; spread chex mixture on paper towels to cool.

Store in airtight containers.

Makes enough to share.

Beverages

Cocoa-Coffee
Mix equal parts of hot cocoa
and hot black coffee, flavor with
vanilla extract and top with
sweetened whipped cream for a delicious fall drink.

Wassail

2 quarts sweet apple cider
2 cups orange juice
1 cup lemon juice
Juice from a No. 2 can pineapple
1 stick whole cinnamon
1 teaspoon whole cloves
Sugar, or honey, to taste

In a large saucepan, combine cider, orange, lemon, and pineapple juices, cinnamon, and cloves. Bring to a simmer.

Taste carefully so as not to burn your mouth. Add sugar or honey; simmer until sugar or honey is dissolved.

Strain through a sieve, lined with a coffee filter or paper towel.

Pour into cups. Serve hot.

Best Ever Punch

5 ripe bananas
2 (12-ounce) cans orange juice concentrate, frozen
1 (46-ounce) can pineapple juice
4 cups sugar
6 cups cold water
7-Up® or ginger ale

Blend bananas and juices in blender. Add sugar and water; blend until well mixed. Pour into container; cover and freeze.

To serve, combine frozen mixture with 7-Up® or ginger ale on a 1-to-1 ratio. Stir until slushy.

Ladle into punch cups. Serves 50.

Gingered Green Tea

12 cups water
½ cup sugar
1 (3-inch) piece fresh ginger, peeled and thinly-sliced
12 green tea bags
Lemon-flavored sparkling water
Slivers of orange, lemon, and lime peel

In a large saucepan, combine water, sugar, and ginger; bring to a boil; reduce heat to a simmer. Cover and simmer 5 minutes; remove from heat.

Add tea bags; cover and let stand 3 minutes. Remove and discard tea bags. Strain tea and discard ginger.

Transfer tea to a 2-gallon pitcher. Cover; let cool. When completely cool, transfer to refrigerator to chill.

For serving, fill glasses with chopped or cubed ice. Add tea to the halfway mark; add sparkling water to fill glass to the top.

Garnish each glass with slivered citrus peel.

Pink Lady Punch

4 cups cranberry juice cocktail
1½ cups granulated sugar
4 cups pineapple juice
2 quarts ginger ale, chilled

Combine cranberry juice and sugar; stir until sugar is dissolved. Add pineapple juice and ginger ale; blend well. Chill in refrigerator. Makes 1 gallon and serves 32.

Double-Lime Punch

1 cup (½-pint) lime sherbet, softened
1 (6-ounce) can frozen limeade concentrate, thawed
2 (7-ounce) bottles ginger ale, chilled
2 cups cold water

Combine all ingredients in a punch bowl; stir until mixed.
Ladle into punch cups. Serves 10.

Mock Champagne Punch

Red and green cherries
Mint leaves
Water
1 quart apple juice
2 large bottles ginger ale
Red food coloring

Make ice cubes with cherries, mint leaves, and water. Freeze.

Just before serving, mix apple juice and ginger ale in a punch bowl with a few drops of red food coloring to make it a light pink.

Ladle punch into glasses over prepared ice cubes. Serves 10-12.

Christmas Punch

5 cups double-strength tea, cooled to room temperature
2¼ cups sugar
2½ cups orange juice
1½ cups grapefruit juice
2/3 cup lemon juice
¼ cup lime juice
1½ quarts ginger ale, chilled
Decorative ice cubes

In a bowl or pitcher, stir tea, sugar, and juices until sugar is dissolved. Cover and chill in refrigerator.

When ready to serve, pour mixture into large pitcher; add ginger ale and decorative ice cubes.

Decorative Ice Cubes

Water
Maraschino cherries, drained
Mint leaves
Pineapple chunks, orange wedges, and/or berries

Fill ice cube tray 1/3 full with water; freeze until partially set. Remove from freezer and add one cherry, mint leaf, and piece of fruit into each cube section. Fill tray with water and freeze.

Breads

Bread (Toast)

Slices should be ½ to ¼ inches thick. Toast should be browned even. Serve hot. It may be buttered at the table; or buttered just before serving and left in oven a few minutes.

Apple Bread

3 cups flour
2 cups sugar
½ teaspoon salt
1 teaspoon baking soda
1 teaspoon cinnamon
½ cup black walnuts
3 eggs
1 ½ cups cooking oil
2 teaspoons vanilla
3 cups raw apples, chopped

Preheat oven to 350°. Grease and flour 2 loaf pans.

Mix flour, sugar, salt, soda, cinnamon and nuts in one bowl. In another bowl, mix eggs, oil, vanilla and apples. Pour egg mixture over dry ingredients and mix well. Pour batter into loaf pans; bake about an hour. Remove bread from oven. After about 10 minutes, remove bread from pans and place on racks to finish cooling.

Apricot Tea Bread

½ cup butter, softened
1 cup sugar
3 eggs
2 teaspoons vanilla
2 cups flour
1½ teaspoons baking powder
1 teaspoon baking soda
1 cup sour cream
1 cup chopped dried apricots
1 cup chopped pecans

For Topping:
½ cup flour
¼ cup sugar
¼ cup cold butter, cut into small cubes

Preheat oven to 350°. Have ready 2 greased 8x4-inch loaf pans.

In a large bowl, cream butter and sugar until light and fluffy. Add eggs, one at a time, beating well after each addition. Beat in vanilla.

Combine flour, baking powder and baking soda; add to creamed mixture alternately with sour cream, beating well after each addition. Fold in apricots and nuts. Spoon batter into prepared loaf pans.

To make topping:

In a small bowl, combine flour and sugar; cut in butter until mixture is crumbly. Sprinkle topping over bread batter.

Bake bread 40-45 minutes or until done. Remove from heat; cool 10 minutes. Remove from pans and cool on wire rack.

Banana Nut Bread

3 ripe bananas
1 cup sugar
1 teaspoon baking soda
1 tablespoon water
2 eggs
1 teaspoon baking powder
1 teaspoon salt
½ cup salad oil
2 cups flour

Peel and mash bananas in a mixing bowl. Add sugar and let stand 15 minutes.

In a small cup, dissolve soda in water; set aside.

Preheat oven to 325°. Grease a 9-inch loaf pan; set aside.

Combine baking powder, salt, and flour; set aside.

Add eggs and soda water to banana mixture; beat well.

Add dry ingredients; stir only until well mixed. Spoon batter into prepared pan and bake 50-60 minutes. Remove pan from oven and let cool slightly. Remove bread from pan to finish cooling on a wire rack.

Variation: May add raisins or nuts to batter.

Pumpkin Bread

3½ cups flour
2 teaspoons baking soda
1½ teaspoons salt
1 teaspoon cinnamon
1 teaspoon nutmeg
3 cups sugar
1 cup pecans, chopped
1 cup cooking oil
4 eggs
2/3 cup water
2 cups canned pumpkin (or cooked and mashed fresh pumpkin)
½ cup chopped dates, optional

Preheat oven to 350°. Grease and floured two 9x5x3-inch loaf pans.

Sift flour, baking soda, salt, cinnamon, nutmeg and sugar into mixing bowl. Add pecans, oil, eggs, water and pumpkin; stir with a spoon until blended. Stir in dates, if desired. Pour into 2 prepared pans. Bake for 1 hour. Let cool in pans for 10 minutes; remove to a cooling rack.

For round loaves, you may bake bread in 4 coffee cans – fill cans ½ full of batter. Can freeze the baked loaves.

Zucchini Squash Bread

2 cups zucchini squash
3 cups flour
1 teaspoon baking soda
1 teaspoon salt
¼ teaspoon baking powder
3 tablespoons cinnamon
3 eggs
2 cups sugar
2 teaspoons vanilla
1 cup nuts, chopped

Preheat oven to 350°.

Grate squash; set aside to drain.

Combine flour, baking soda, salt, baking powder, and cinnamon; set aside.

In a large mixing bowl, beat sugar and eggs. Stir in vanilla and squash. Add dry ingredients; mix well. Stir in nuts. Pour batter into prepared pans.

Bake for 45-55 minutes. Remove from oven and cool slightly. Remove bread from pans to finish cooling on a wire rack.

Aunt Lucy's Monkey Bread

4 cans ready-to-bake biscuits
1 stick margarine
¾ cup granulated sugar
4 tablespoons cinnamon
¼ cup packed brown sugar

Preheat oven to 350°.
Mix sugar and cinnamon; set aside.
Open biscuit tubes and remove biscuits. Cut into ¼-inch pieces. Roll, or shake, biscuit pieces in sugar and cinnamon. Pack pieces into a greased tube cake pan.
Melt margarine with brown sugar. Pour mixture over biscuits.
Bake 35-40 minutes.
Turn pan upside down to release bread onto a platter. Serve bread as is; do not turn it over.

Raisin-Nut Monkey Bread

¾ cup granulate sugar
2 teaspoons cinnamon
3 (12-ounce) rolls refrigerated biscuit dough
½ cup chopped walnuts
½ cup raisins
½ cup margarine, melted
1 cup packed brown sugar

Preheat oven to 350°. Grease a Bundt or tube pan.
Mix granulated sugar and cinnamon in a large plastic bag. Cut biscuits into quarters. Shake 8 biscuit pieces in bag; arrange pieces in bottom of prepared pan. Place nuts and raisins among biscuit pieces as you build uneven layers with more sugared biscuit pieces, continuing until all nuts, raisins, and biscuit pieces are used. Boil margarine and brown sugar in small saucepan for 1 minute; pour over top of biscuits. Bake 35 minutes; let cool in pan 10 minutes but no longer. Turn out onto a plate. Self-serve; pull pieces apart

Old-Fashioned White Bread

1 cup + 2 tablespoons milk (90-100°F)
3 cups all-purpose white flour (or bread flour
2 tablespoons sugar
1½ teaspoons salt
2 tablespoons butter or margarine
2 teaspoons active dry yeast (or 1½ teaspoons bread machine/fast-rise yeast)

Pour liquid ingredients into pan of bread maker.

Add dry ingredients, except yeast, to pan. Tap pan to settle dry ingredients.

Cut butter or margarine into four pieces and place into corners of pan.

Make a well in center of dry ingredients; spoon yeast into well.

Place pan in bread maker and lock in place.

Program bread maker for BASIC/SPECIALTY and MEDIUM bread color.

Start bread maker. (Mine takes 3 hours 10 minutes to mix, rise twice, and bake. Set it and forget it.)

When done, turn off bread maker; remove bread from pan and let cool on rack before slicing.

These two recipes came from a home economics course in the 1940s. My mother and two aunts (her sister and my father's sister) all took the course at the same time.

Bread Muffins

2 cups flour
2 tablespoons sugar
2 ½ teaspoons baking powder
½ teaspoon salt
1 cup milk
1 egg
2 tablespoons shortening, melted

Preheat oven to 400°. Grease muffin tins.

In a bowl, sift flour, sugar, baking powder, and salt; set aside. In a small bowl, beat milk and egg together. Add dry ingredients and shortening; mix thoroughly.

Fill muffin tins half full.

Bake for 20-25 minutes.

Serve hot.

Sour-Milk Biscuits

2 cups flour
2 teaspoons baking powder
1 teaspoon salt
¼ teaspoon baking soda
2/3 cup milk
2 tablespoons shortening, melted

Preheat oven to 400°. Grease a baking pan.

In a bowl, sift flour, baking powder, salt, and baking soda. Add milk and shortening; mix thoroughly.

Roll out dough and cut into rounds.

Bake for 20-25 minutes.

Serve hot.

If you love English muffins, you'll really like this bread. English muffins are way too time-consuming to make at home, and store-bought muffins never taste fresh enough. This dough is simple to make.

English Muffin Bread

3 cups milk
5 cups bread flour
4½ teaspoons instant, or rapid-rise, yeast
2 teaspoons salt
1 tablespoon sugar
1 teaspoon baking soda
Grease and cornmeal, for pans

Warm milk in a small pan to 120° F.

In a large bowl, combine flour, yeast, salt, sugar, and baking soda. Add milk; stir quickly until combined. Cover dough with a greased plastic wrap; let rise in a warm place for 30 minutes or until doubled.

Grease 2 9-inch loaf pans and dust with cornmeal.

Heat oven to 375°.

Stir down dough; divide in half; put dough into prepared pans, working it into corners with your thumb. Cover bread dough with greased plastic wrap; let rise 30 minutes or until the pans are full.

Bake 30 minutes or until loaves are browned. Remove pans from oven; flip bread loaves onto a wire rack to cool.

To serve, slice and toast. Spread with butter and jam, scrambled eggs, or whatever you like on regular English muffins.

Cheese and Chili Cornbread

3 eggs
1 (8-ounce) can whole kernel corn, drained
1 (4-ounce) can chopped green chilies
1 cup yellow cornmeal
1 teaspoon salt
1½ tablespoons baking powder
1 cup sour cream
¼ cup margarine, melted
¼ pound grated Monterey Jack cheese
Butter

Preheat oven to 350°.

Have ready a lightly-greased 9-inch square baking pan.

In a large bowl, beat eggs slightly. Add corn and chilies; mix well. Stir in cornmeal, salt, baking powder, sour cream, margarine, and cheese. When blended, pour into prepared pan.

Bake 40 minutes, or until golden on top and a cake tester inserted in its center comes out clean. Remove from oven.

Cut into squares. Serve hot with butter.

Salads

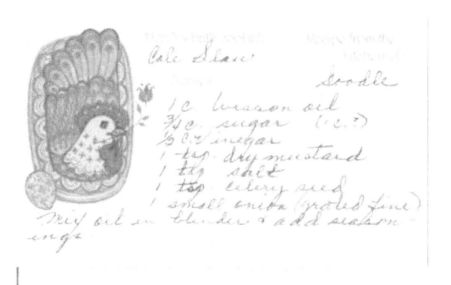

Note: As you can see, the recipe lacks the all-important shredded cabbage, and the sugar has been increased to 1 cup.

Sweet Potato and Spinach Salad

1 egg white
1 tablespoon Worcestershire sauce
½ pound pecan halves
1 tablespoon brown sugar, packed
½ teaspoon salt
3 medium-sized sweet potatoes, peeled and cubed
¼ teaspoon black pepper mixed with ¼ teaspoon salt
2 tablespoons olive oil
8 cups baby spinach
1 cup dried cranberries

Preheat oven to 375°. Spray a large, heavy jellyroll pan (or shallow roasting pan) with cooking spray; set aside.

Whisk egg white in a bowl until frothy; whisk in Worcestershire sauce. Add pecans; stir to coat. Pour pecans into a colander; drain off excess egg white. Return pecans to bowl and add brown sugar and ½ teaspoon salt; stir well to coat each pecan half. Pour pecans in prepared pan; spread out for an even layer. Roast in oven for 5 minutes; stir pecans; roast another 5 minutes; stir pecans. Turn off oven, leaving pecans inside to roast 5-10 minutes longer. Remove pecans from oven and cool on parchment paper.

Preheat oven to 425°. Using the same pan, toss potatoes with olive oil, and pepper and salt mixture. Roast for 25 minutes, until tender.

Make special vinaigrette while potatoes roast. In a large salad bowl, have spinach, cranberries, and 1 cup pecans ready to add to cooked potatoes; toss with vinaigrette, Start with 1/3 cup dressing, adding more if needed.

*Note: See next page for **Vinaigrette Dressing for Sweet Potato Salad.***

Vinaigrette Dressing for Sweet Potato Salad

¼ cup red onion, chopped fine
1 tablespoon red wine vinegar
2 tablespoons lemon juice
3 tablespoons creole mustard
½ teaspoon salt
2 tablespoons brown sugar, packed
¾ cup olive oil

Place onion, vinegar, juice, mustard, salt, and sugar in a blender jar; blend until mixed. With blender on medium speed, slowly drizzle oil into mixture, blending to emulsify the dressing.

Quick Salad for Two

1 cup broccoli, chopped fine
1 carrot, shredded
1 rib celery, chopped
¼ cup red onion, diced
¼ cup dried cranberries
1 cup cauliflower, chopped fine (optional)
3-4 tablespoons bottled coleslaw dressing
¼ cup pecans, roughly-chopped
Salt and pepper to taste

In small salad bowl, combine broccoli, carrot, celery, onion, and cranberries. Add cauliflower, if using. Pour dressing over vegetables; toss to coat. Cover bowl and chill.

Garnish with pecans and serve, sprinkling with salt and pepper, as needed.

Note: Refrigerated salad keeps for several days and travels well for lunch at work.

Bow-Tie Pasta Salad

2½ cups broccoli, chopped
½ cup carrots, shredded
1½ cups celery, chopped
2/3 cup red onion, chopped fine
2/3 cup frozen green peas, thawed
2 cups cooked bow-tie pasta, drained and cooled
½ teaspoon salt
¼ teaspoon black pepper
Bottled coleslaw dressing
1½ cups green grapes, halved
½ cup pecans, chopped
Fresh spinach, spring greens, or mixed greens (optional)

In large bowl, combine broccoli, carrots, celery, onion, peas, pasta, salt, and pepper. Add enough dressing to coat. Fold in grapes. Top with pecans. Cover bowl and chill.

Serve as is as a side dish for sandwiches.

Or serve over a bed of spinach and greens for a dinner salad.

Variations:
1. Skip the pecans and top salad with chopped, roasted chicken atop your choice of fresh greens.
2. For an all green salad, skip the carrots, substitute scallions for the red onion and choose spinach bow-tie or fusilli pasta noodles. (Save the orange and white noodles for something else if you bought multi-color pasta packages.) Serve pasta salad atop a bed of greens. Great for Saint Patrick's Day.
3. Or, add a pop of red with dried cranberries to the all-green salad during the Christmas season.)

Mexican Bean Salad

1 (15-ounce) can black beans, rinsed and drained
1 (15-ounce) can kidney beans, rinsed and drained
1 (15-ounce) can cannellini beans, rinsed and drained
1 green bell pepper, chopped
1 red bell pepper, chopped
1 (10-ounce) package frozen corn kernels, thawed
1 red onion, chopped
½ cup olive oil
½ cup red wine vinegar
2 tablespoons fresh lime juice
1 tablespoon fresh lemon juice
2 tablespoons sugar
1 tablespoon salt
1 clove garlic, crushed
¼ cup chopped fresh cilantro
½ tablespoon ground cumin
½ teaspoon black pepper
½ teaspoon chili powder
Dash hot pepper sauce

In a very large bowl, combine beans, bell peppers, corn kernels, and onion; set aside.

Make dressing. In a small bowl, combine olive oil, vinegar, lime and lemon juices, sugar, salt, garlic, cilantro, cumin, black pepper, chili powder, and hot sauce. Whisk until well blended.

Pour dressing over salad; mix with spatula or large spoon.

Cover and place in refrigerator to chill and marinate.

To serve, toss salad.

Can also be served at room temperature after first chilling.

Italian Crunchy Salad

1 red bell pepper
1 green bell pepper
1 cucumber
1 zucchini
1 yellow summer squash
1 carrot
1 red onion, sliced very thin
3 cups cauliflower florets
4 cups broccoli florets
2 packages Italian salad dressing mix
¼ cup red wine vinegar
¼ cup olive oil
1 teaspoon salt
½ teaspoon black pepper
3-4 cups cooked and cooled fusilli pasta

Wash, but do not dry, bell peppers, cucumber, zucchini, summer squash, and carrot; chop into bite-sized pieces. Place all into a very large bowl. Add onion, cauliflower, and broccoli. Sprinkle dry seasoning mixes over vegetables; toss to coat. Cover bowl and refrigerate at least 4 hours.

In a small bowl, mix vinegar, oil, salt, and black pepper. Pour over vegetables in bowl; toss to coat. Add pasta noodles; toss gently until coated.

Serve chilled.

Note: Makes a large salad – great for picnics or potluck. Can be kept at room temperature for a short period of time.

Tuna and Apple Salad

2 apples, chopped
Juice of ½ lemon
1 ½ cups celery, diced
2 cups canned tuna, flaked
¾ cup mayonnaise
Iceberg lettuce
Pimento, if desired

Sprinkle apples with lemon juice. Add celery and tuna; toss; add mayonnaise and mix lightly. Arrange on a bed of lettuce. Garnish with strips of pimento.

Orange-Cauliflower Salad

2 cups cauliflower, separated into small florets
¼ cup green pepper, chopped
2 cups baby spinach leaves
2 cans mandarin oranges, drained
½ cup poppy seed salad dressing

Combine all ingredients in a salad bowl and serve.
Serves 6.

Avocado-Grapefruit Salad

1 ripe avocado
Salt
Lemon juice
1 grapefruit
Poppy seed salad dressing

Cut avocado in half, remove seed, and peel halves. Cut into ¼-inch slices; sprinkle with salt and lemon juice. Set aside.

Peel and section grapefruit or substitute canned grapefruit. Arrange avocado and grapefruit on lettuce. Drizzle with dressing.

Serves 4.

Note: Bottled poppy seed dressing is available, but a recipe for it is included in this cookbook.

24-Hour Vegetable Salad

4 cups fresh greens (iceberg, Bibb, Boston, or leaf lettuce,
romaine, spinach leaves, or a combination of any of these)
Salt and pepper
1 cup fresh mushrooms, sliced
¾ cup broccoli florets
½ cup frozen peas
1 cup carrots, shredded
2 eggs, hard-cooked and sliced
6 slices bacon, cooked crisp, drained, and crumbled
¼ cup green onions, sliced thin
¾ cup (3 ounces) Colby, cheddar, or Swiss cheese
¾ cup mayonnaise
1 tablespoon lemon juice
Dill seasoning or fresh dill (optional)

In a large salad bowl, tear greens and cover bottom of bowl.
Sprinkle salt and pepper to taste. Layer the following, in order, on
top of greens: mushrooms, broccoli, peas, carrots, eggs, bacon,
onions, and 2 ounces of cheese.

In a small bowl, combine mayonnaise, lemon juice, and dill, if
used; mix well. Spread dressing on salad. Sprinkle with remaining
cheese.

Cover bowl tightly with plastic wrap and place in refrigerator to
chill for 2-24 hours.

To serve, remove from refrigerator and toss salad to coat
vegetables with dressing. Serves 6-8.

Macaroni Salad

8 ounces elbow macaroni,
½ pound green beans, cut into 1-inch pieces
¼ cup lemon juice
1 tablespoon Dijon mustard
1 teaspoon salt
¼ teaspoon pepper
1/3 cup salad or olive oil
1/3 cup yogurt
1¼ cups (5 ounces) cheddar cheese, cubed
1 cup baby spinach leaves
1 large tomato, seeded and chopped
½ cup green onions, chopped

Cook macaroni, following directions on the package. During the last five minutes of cooking, add green beans. Drain and rinse with cold water; set aside.

In a salad bowl, whisk together lemon juice, mustard, salt, and pepper. Gradually whisk in oil. Whisk in yogurt. Add cheese, spinach, tomato, onions, macaroni and green beans. Toss and serve.

Tossed salad may be covered and refrigerated up to 24 hours.

Pasta Slaw

1 (7-ounce) package ditalini or elbow noodles
1 small carrot
1 large onion
2 celery ribs
1 cucumber
1 green bell pepper
1 (8-ounce) can water chestnuts, drained
1 (14-ounce) package coleslaw mix

Cook pasta, as directed on the package. While it's cooking, chop carrot, onion, celery, cucumber, bell pepper, and water chestnuts; place in a very large bowl. Reserve a little bit of carrot and bell pepper for garnish.

Drain pasta; rinse with cold water; drain again. Add pasta and coleslaw mix to bowl with vegetables; set aside.

Make dressing; pour over salad and toss well. Cover and chill salad and garnish a minimum of 1 hour.

At serving, garnish with carrot and bell pepper.

Simple Dressing

¼ cup apple cider vinegar
1½ cups mayonnaise
1/3 cup sugar
½ teaspoon salt
¼ teaspoon black pepper

Mix all ingredients in a small bowl; pour over salad.

Beet Salad

¾ cup walnuts, chopped and toasted
2 large carrots, peeled and sliced in thin strips
2 medium beets, peeled and sliced in thin rounds
1 bag (5-6 ounces) spring greens or arugula
1 tablespoon red onion, chopped fine
¼ cup lemon juice
1 teaspoon Dijon mustard
½ cup olive or salad oil
1 tablespoon brown sugar, packed
1/8 teaspoon black pepper
1/8 teaspoon salt

In a small bowl, whisk together: onion, lemon juice, mustard, oil, brown sugar, pepper, and salt.

In a medium-sized bowl, toss greens with dressing. Using tongs, remove greens to platter, arranging in an even layer. Toss carrots and beets in dressing; remove them and place on top of greens.

To serve, sprinkle salad with nuts.

Note: When working with beets or other foods that can stain your hands, wear plastic or vinyl gloves. Drug stores and major retailers carry medical and/or food service gloves.

Spinach Salad

1 package fresh spinach leaves
3 hard-boiled eggs, sliced
8 slices bacon, fried crisp and crumbled
1 small red onion, sliced into thin rings
½ pound cheddar cheese
½ cup mayonnaise
½ bacon grease, at room temperature
(May substitute vegetable or olive oil for bacon grease, if desired)

In a large salad bowl, place spinach, eggs, bacon, onion, and cheese. In a small bowl, stir mayonnaise and grease, or oil, until blended. Pour over spinach mixture and toss salad.

Wilted Lettuce

6 slices bacon
½ cup sliced green onion
¼ cup apple cider vinegar
¼ cup water
4 teaspoons sugar
¼ teaspoon salt
8 cups leaf lettuce, torn in bite-size pieces
6 radishes, sliced thin
1 hard-boiled egg, chopped

In a skillet, cook bacon until crisp; remove bacon from skillet. Crumble bacon and set aside.

Add onion to bacon drippings in skillet; cook until onion is tender. Add vinegar, water, sugar, and salt; cook and stir until mixture comes to a boil. Return crumbled bacon to skillet; stir in.

Put lettuce in a very large bowl. Pour bacon dressing over lettuce and toss to coat.

Garnish with radishes and egg.

Serve immediately.

Bacon-Broccoli Salad

4 slices bacon
2 crowns broccoli florets
3 green onions, sliced thin
¾ cup dried cranberries
3 tablespoons salad oil
3 tablespoons rice vinegar
2 tablespoons sugar
½ cup sunflower kernels

In a skillet, fry bacon until crisp; drain; crumble, and set aside.

In a large salad bowl, combine broccoli, onions, and cranberries. In a small jar with a tight-fitting lid, combine oil, vinegar, and sugar; shake well until sugar is dissolved. Pour dressing over broccoli mixture; toss to coat. Cover bowl with plastic wrap and refrigerate.

To serve, toss salad mixture again and top with bacon and sunflower kernels.

Colorful Salad

1 cup green beans, cooked to crisp-tender
1 cup corn kernels, cooked to crisp-tender
1 cup frozen green peas, thawed
¾ cup shredded carrot
½ cup chopped celery
¼ cup chopped red onion
½ cup chopped yellow bell pepper
½ cup chopped orange bell pepper
½ cup chopped red bell pepper
½ cup chopped and seeded cucumber
1 tomato, seeded and coarsely chopped
1 tablespoon granulated sugar
1 teaspoon salt
½ teaspoon black pepper
1 tablespoon olive oil
1 tablespoon red wine vinegar
1 package of greens (optional)

In a large salad bowl, combine green beans, corn, peas, carrot, celery, onion, bell peppers, cucumber, and tomato.

In a small jar, combine sugar, salt, black pepper, olive oil, and vinegar. Cover jar and shake until ingredients are well mixed. Pour dressing over vegetable salad; toss to coat.

Serve as is or over a bed of greens – your choice of spring mix, spinach leaves, or leaf lettuce. Romaine or iceberg lettuce may be used, but the vegetable colors pop when the leaves are dark.

Angel Slaw

1 (10-ounce) package angel hair coleslaw mix
1 cup dried cranberries
1 cup sliced almonds, toasted
¾ cup poppy seed salad dressing
½ teaspoon salt
¼ teaspoon black pepper

In a large salad bowl, combine cabbage, cranberries, and nuts. Drizzle salad dressing over mixture and sprinkle with salt and pepper. Toss salad to coat. Cover bowl with plastic wrap and place in refrigerator to chill for at least one hour before serving.

Potluck Cauliflower-Broccoli-Raisin Salad

3 cups cauliflower florets
6 cups broccoli florets
½ cup raisins
½ cup walnuts, toasted and rough-chopped
¼ cup salad or olive oil
¼ cup apple cider vinegar
1 teaspoon sugar
½ teaspoon black pepper

In a steamer, steam all florets until crisp-tender, or boil cauliflower and broccoli for 2 minutes in boiling water in separate covered saucepans; drain and rinse with cold water.

In a salad bowl, layer half the cauliflower, broccoli, raisins, and walnuts. Repeat with another layer. Cover bowl with plastic wrap and chill in refrigerator.

For dressing, combine oil, vinegar, sugar, and pepper in a jar with a tight-fitting lid; shake well.

At potluck location, shake dressing, pour over salad, and toss to coat. Serves 10.

Red and White Bean Salad

2 (15-ounce cans) red kidney beans, drained
2 (16-ounce) cans white kidney beans, drained
1 large onion, sliced thin
½ cup diced celery
1/3 cup vegetable oil
½ cup apple cider vinegar
½ teaspoon dry mustard
½ teaspoon garlic salt
¼ teaspoon black pepper

In a large bowl, combine beans, onion, and celery; set aside.

In a small bowl, combine oil, vinegar, dry mustard, garlic salt, and black pepper; blend thoroughly. Pour dressing over beat mixture; toss lightly. Cover and chill.

Serves 8.

Chicken and Baby Corn Salad

2 cups cooked chicken
1 (6-7 ounce) rice pilaf mix
1 (14-ounce) can whole baby corn, drained
½ chopped red bell pepper
½ cup fresh snow peas, sliced
½ cup thin slices celery
¼ cup sliced green onions
½ cup bottled Asian salad dressing
Toasted sesame seeds
Soy sauce

Shred cooked chicken; set aside. Prepare the rice pilaf mix, following directions on the package; set aside.

In a large bowl, combine chicken, baby corn, bell pepper, snow peas, celery, and onions. Stir in cooked rice. Add salad dressing; stir gently to combine.

At serving time, sprinkle salad with sesame seeds. Provide dipping bowls of soy sauce.

Sliced-Pepper Salad

1 yellow bell pepper
1 orange bell pepper
1 red bell pepper
1 green bell pepper
1 yellow onion
1 large cucumber
2 tomatoes
2 small radishes
½ cup vegetable or olive oil
1/3 cup red wine vinegar
2 teaspoons sugar
1 teaspoon salt
½ teaspoon black pepper
½ teaspoon dried oregano
Fresh parsley and basil (optional)

Core and seed four bell peppers; slice into very thin slices. Peel onion, cut in half and slice thinly. Peel and seed cucumber; cut into thirds and slice thinly. Core and seed tomatoes; cut each in half and slice thinly. Clean radishes and slice very thin.

In a large glass or plastic bowl, combine bell peppers, onion, cucumber, tomatoes, and radishes. In a small mixing bowl, combine oil, vinegar, sugar, salt, black pepper, and oregano; whisk until it is thoroughly blended. Pour dressing over bell pepper mix; gently toss with a spatula. Cover and marinate 1-2 hours at room temperature.

Garnish with fresh parsley and basil Serve at room temperature.

Note: By serving at room temperature, this is a great salad for a buffet or picnic. To make ahead or keep as a left over, cover and refrigerate.

If you own a mandoline, drag it out. Good excuse to use it

This salad works well with any meal but is especially good for brunch, prepared the night before and served as a side dish to **Breakfast Casserole**.

Frozen Cranberry Salad

1 can whole cranberry sauce
1 small carton sour cream
1 small can crushed pineapple, drained
1 handful chopped pecans

In a small bowl, beat cranberry sauce and sour cream with a spoon. Add pineapple and pecans; pour mixture into a glass baking pan. Cover and place in freezer until firm. Serve frozen.

Wheat Berry Waldorf Salad

2½ cups water
¾ cup wheat berries, rinsed
1/3 cup olive oil
¼ cup snipped fresh parsley
¼ cup apple cider vinegar
¼ cup apple juice
2 tablespoons sugar
1 teaspoon salt
½ teaspoon ground cinnamon
1 Granny Smith apple, unpeeled, cored, chopped
1 Braeburn or Rome apple, unpeeled, cored, and chopped
1 stalk celery, chopped fine
½ cup dried cranberries
½ cup seedless red or green grapes, halved
6-8 Bibb or Boston lettuce leaves
Honey roasted peanuts

In a small bowl, combine water and wheat berries. Cover and chill for 6 to 24 hours; do not drain. Transfer to a medium saucepan. Bring to boiling; reduce heat. Cover pan and simmer 30 minutes, or until wheat berries are tender with a firm, chewy texture. Drain; transfer to a bowl to cool.

In a quart jar, combine, oil, parsley, vinegar, juice, sugar, salt, and cinnamon; cover and shake well to combine. Drizzle dressing over warm wheat berries; stir to coat.

In a large bowl, combine apples, celery, cranberries, and grapes. Stir in wheat berry mixture; mix well.

Serve immediately or cover and chill for up to 4 hours.

To serve, arrange lettuce leaves on a large platter or divide them among individual salad plates. Spoon salad into the lettuce leaves. Sprinkle with nuts.

Two-Tone Salad

1 small package lemon Jello®
1 small package orange Jello®
2 cups boiling water
1½ cups cold water
1 (#2) can crushed pineapple, drained (save juice)
1 can mandarin oranges, drained
2 bananas
1 egg
2 tablespoons margarine
2 tablespoons flour
½ cup sugar
2 cups whipping cream

Mix lemon and orange powders with boiling water. When powder is dissolved, add cold water and stir. Pour into a glass pan. Chill until just starting to gel. Remove pan from refrigerator; stir in pineapple and oranges. Slice bananas; stir into gel mixture. Return pan to refrigerator to chill completely.

Make topping:
Measure pineapple juice; add water, if needed to make 1 cup.
In a saucepan, combine pineapple juice, egg, margarine, flour, and sugar. Cook, stirring constantly, until thickened. Remove from heat and cool slightly. Fold in whipped topping.
Spread topping over chilled salad.

Ruth's Jello® Salad

1 large box Raspberry Jello®
1 cup boiling water
1 (15-ounce) can crushed pineapple, drained
1 can blueberry pie filling

Have on hand an 8x8-inch square pan.
In a bowl, mix Jello® with water until dissolved; let cool.
When cooled, add pineapple and pie filling. Stir well and pour into pan. Cover and place in refrigerator; chill until set.
Make topping recipe. (see below)

Whipped Topping

1 (8-ounce) package cream cheese
1 medium-sized tub Cool Whip®
1 cup powdered sugar

In a mixing bowl, combine cream cheese, whipped topping, and powdered sugar. Using a hand mixer on low setting, mix until well blended.
Spread topping over top of chilled salad like icing a cake. Cover and refrigerate until ready to serve.

Ribbon Salad

2 (3-ounce) boxes lime Jello
Water
1 (3-ounce) box lemon Jello
1 (8-ounce) package cream cheese
¼ pound miniature marshmallows
1 can crushed pineapple, drained
1 cup whipped topping
2 (3-ounce) boxes cherry Jello

In a bowl, mix lime Jello with 2 cups hot water; stir in 2 cups cold water; pour mixture into 9x13-inch glass pan. Place in refrigerator to harden.

In another bowl, mix lemon Jello with 1 cup hot water. Add cream cheese and marshmallows into hot Jello; stir until creamy. Place bowl in refrigerator to let mixture set partially. Remove bowl from refrigerator; add pineapple and whipped topping; blend well.

Remove pan from refrigerator and pour lemon mixture over lime Jello. Return pan to refrigerator.

In one more bowl, mix cherry Jello with 2 cups hot water; stir in 2 cups cold water. Refrigerate until cool and starting to gel.

Remove pan and cherry Jello bowl from refrigerator and spread cherry mixture over first two layers.

Return pan to refrigerator to chill salad and let set completely. Cut into squares to serve.

Ranch Dressing

1 tablespoon onion, grated
1 clove garlic, grated
2 tablespoons parsley, minced
1/3 cup celery leaves, minced
¼ cup buttermilk
¾ cup mayonnaise
¼ teaspoon celery seed
¼ teaspoon thyme
¼ teaspoon salt
1/8 teaspoon black pepper

Combine all ingredients in a small bowl; mix well. Cover and refrigerate. Yield: about 1½ cups. (Stays fresh several days.)

French Dressing

1 cup salad oil
½ cup apple cider vinegar
1 can tomato soup
¼ cup sugar
Dash of paprika
Dash of garlic salt

Combine all ingredients in a quart jar with a tight-fitting lid. Cover and shake until thoroughly mixed. Refrigerate dressing. Yield: about 3 cups.

Main Dishes

Here's what's cookin' Ham Supreme Serves
Recipe from the kitchen of B Shepherd
Cream of Onion Soup
½ can milk
2 T. Miracle Whip
½ can Fr. Fried Onions
Cooked noodles
Peas
Cubed Ham
Pimiento
½ cup cheddar cheese
Salt, Pepper, Garlic Salt, Worcestershire
sauce, Parsley

Chicken-Fried Steak

1 large egg
¼ cup milk
Round steak, sliced thin and tenderized
Flour
Saltine cracker crumbs
Vegetable shortening or bacon grease

Beat egg and milk together in glass pie pan. Put flour in another pie pan and cracker crumbs in a third pie pan. Dredge steaks, one at a time, into flour, then dip into egg mixture, then into cracker crumbs, pressing crumbs into meat. Set aside on waxed paper or a plate until all are coated. Melt shortening in a large skillet; brown steaks on both sides; and then simmer over very low heat for 15-30 minutes, depending on thickness of meat, or deep-fry meat at 380° in skillet until done. Remove steaks from skillet and drain on paper towels. Serve steak hot with cream gravy.

Variation:
Add ¾ cup buttermilk to egg and milk mixture. Eliminate the cracker crumbs. Dip steaks in flour, then in egg-milk mixture, and then back in flour. Fry steaks in grease over medium-high heat until browned, about 3 minutes per side. Let drain on paper towels.

Cream Gravy

To make cream gravy, use equal amounts fat and flour. Usual amount is 3 tablespoons pan drippings, bacon grease, or vegetable shortening to 3 tablespoons all-purpose flour. Stir in hot skillet until flour is lightly-browned. Add about 2 cups whole milk and bring to a boil; stir constantly until thickened, about 2 minutes. Add salt and pepper, to taste.

For the milk, you can substitute equal amounts water and evaporated milk or 1 cup heavy cream and 1 cup beef broth. If the gravy gets too thick, add a small amount of milk or water.

Easy-Beef Fajitas

2 pounds beef steak
1 packet fajita or taco seasoning
1 large onion
2 bell peppers
2 tablespoons ketchup
½ cup water

Have on hand at serving time:
Tortillas
Guacamole
Shredded cheese
Shredded iceberg lettuce
1 tomato, coarsely chopped
Sour cream

Cut steak, onion, and peppers into thin strips. Place in slow cooker; sprinkle with seasoning packet; add ketchup and water. Cover and cook on low setting 6-8 hours (or 4-6 hours on high setting) until meat is tender.

To serve: Spoon meat mixture onto tortillas; top with guacamole, cheese, lettuce, tomato, and sour cream.

Citrusy Chicken Fajitas

6 tablespoons lemon juice
¼ cup lime juice
2 tablespoons minced cilantro
1 tablespoon olive oil
1 teaspoon sugar
½ teaspoon garlic powder
½ teaspoon cumin
1 pound boneless skinless chicken breasts, cut into strips
1 green bell pepper
1 red bell pepper
1 yellow bell pepper
1 large red onion, sliced thin
4 (8-inch) flour tortillas
½ cup shredded lettuce
¼ cup ripe olives, sliced
¼ cup shredded cheddar cheese

In a small bowl, combine first seven ingredients. Divide marinade between two large plastic bags; add chicken one bag, peppers and onion to other. Seal bags; massage to coat ingredients; refrigerate several hours or overnight.

Drain chicken and vegetables; discard all marinade. In a large nonstick skillet, spray with cooking spray and cook chicken over medium heat 3 minutes, stirring. Add onion and peppers; cook 3-5 minutes or until chicken is done and peppers are crisp-tender. Remove from heat.

To serve, spoon filling onto warmed tortillas; top with lettuce olives and cheese.

Jennifer Eve shared this recipe and says you may substitute a purchased rotisserie chicken to save time. When boiling a whole chicken, she debones the chicken and uses the carcass to make homemade chicken stock – see her Chicken and Wild Rice Soup for directions.

Chicken Enchilada Casserole

1 whole chicken
1 can cream of celery soup (98%fat free)
1 can cream of chicken soup (98% fat free)
1 can cream of mushroom soup (98% fat free)
1 (4-ounce) can diced green chilies
1 jalapeno, diced
1 onion, diced
12 flour tortillas, quartered
3 cups reduced-fat Mexican cheese blend
¼ cup skim milk
1(4-ounce) can chopped black olives
Iceberg lettuce, tomatoes, and salsa

In large pan with water, bring chicken to a boil; reduce heat and simmer until done. Remove from heat. When cool, shred chicken.

In a saucepan, mix the three soups, can of green chilies, jalapeno, and onion; cook until bubbly. Add the shredded chicken to half of the soup mixture.

Heat oven to 350°.

In a 13 x 9 inch pan, layer:

Chicken/soup mixture,

Quartered flour tortillas, arranged to cover,

Some of the cheese, sprinkled over tortillas.

Repeat the layers.

Add the milk to the rest of the soup mixture, then pour on top as the sauce. Top with the rest of the cheese, then the diced olives.

Bake, uncovered, for 30-45 minutes, until the cheese is bubbly.

Eve tops individual servings of the casserole with shredded iceberg lettuce, diced tomatoes, and of course, salsa!

This is one of Jo Thomas Eve's most-requested recipes. Jennifer says it's great with a salad and fruit for dinner.

Beef Enchilada Casserole

2 pounds ground beef
1 onion, diced
1 tablespoon minced garlic
1 can enchilada sauce
2 cans cream of mushroom soup
1 can diced green chilies
18 corn tortillas
1 cup grated cheese

Preheat oven to 350°.

Brown ground beef with onion and garlic in large skillet. Add enchilada sauce.

In a medium saucepan, combine soup and green chilies; heat until bubbly.

Layer in a 13x9-inch pan: 1/2 meat mixture, cover with 6 tortillas, and 1/2 soup mixture. Cover that with 6 tortillas, remaining meat mixture, last 6 tortillas, and remaining soup mixture. Top with grated cheese.

Bake 30-45 minutes.

Busy Day Meal

4 boneless pork loin chops
1 tablespoon bacon grease or olive oil
1 can condensed tomato soup
1 cup water
1 teaspoon salt
1 teaspoon seasoned salt
½ teaspoon black pepper
1 teaspoon parsley flakes
1½ teaspoons Worcestershire sauce
2 tablespoons chopped onion
5 carrots, sliced in 1½-inch pieces
6 medium potatoes, quartered

Preheat oven to 375°.

Brown chops in bacon grease in a skillet; remove chops to a plate. In a small bowl, mix soup, water, salts, pepper, parsley, Worcestershire sauce, and onion until smooth; set aside.

In a 2-quart covered casserole dish, place carrots in bottom and cover carrots with potatoes. Place pork chops on top of potatoes. Pour soup mixture over meat and vegetables.

Cover casserole dish and place in oven. Bake for 1 hour and 15 minutes, or until meat is tender and vegetables are done. Remove from oven; let cool a few minutes before serving.

Variation: **Busy Day Ribs**

Soak 3 pounds farmer-style pork ribs in salt water for 2 hours; remove ribs from water. Brown ribs in skillet. Place carrots in slow cooker; cover with potatoes and ribs. Prepare soup mixture as above, but add an additional can tomato soup. Pour over meat and vegetables. Cover and cook on high 6-8 hours or until meat and vegetables are tender.

One of my former supervisors shares my passion of collecting books and cookbooks. Where I'm a home cook, he's more of a gourmet cook. He shares this recipe for my cookbook.

Chicken Cacciatore a la Gary Clark

4 tablespoons olive oil
1 medium red onion, chopped
3-3½ pound boneless chicken
1 cup flour
2 teaspoons salt
½ teaspoon black pepper
2½ cups tomatoes, chopped
½ cup green bell pepper, chopped
1 clove garlic
½ cup white wine
Cooked spaghetti

In a large skillet, brown onion pieces in 2 tablespoons oil. Remove onions from pan; set aside. Coat chicken in flour, salt and pepper. Add remaining 2 tablespoons oil to oil in skillet; sauté chicken until brown. Add tomatoes, green pepper garlic and browned onions to skillet. Cover and simmer for 15 minutes. Uncover skillet and add wine; re-cover and simmer 20 more minutes. Remove pan from heat and serve chicken mixture over spaghetti with glasses of Gallo Hearty Burgundy®.

Snapper with Fennel

1 lime
1 large fennel bulb
1 teaspoon fennel seeds
Water
¼ teaspoon salt
4 teaspoons olive oil, divided
2 garlic cloves, minced
4 fish fillets (snapper, sole, or striped bass)

Grate ¾ teaspoon zest from lime peel. Cut lime in half. Reserve one half for garnish, slicing it in 4 slices. Squeeze juice from other half of lime into small cup. Set all aside.

Slice fennel bulb in ¼-inch slices. Chop 1 tablespoon from fennel fronds. Set aside.

Dry-toast fennel seeds for 1-2 minutes in a small saute pan over medium heat. Remove from heat and let cool. Grind seeds with mortar and pestle, spice grinder, or mini food processor.

Bring 1-inch of water to a boil in a large saucepan. Add fennel slices and salt; cover and boil until crisp-tender, about 6-8 minutes. Drain fennel and pat dry.

Add 2 teaspoons olive oil and cooked fennel to a large skillet; saute for 3 minutes. Add garlic; cook another minute or two until fennel begins to brown. Remove food from skillet and set aside.

Add remaining 2 teaspoons olive oil to same skillet; warm over medium-high heat. Add fish fillets 3-4 minutes per side. Remove fillets from pan when fish flakes with a fork.

Drizzle fillets with lime juice; sprinkle with fennel seeds and lime zest.

Serve fish over bed of fennel, garnished with lime slices and fennel fronds.

Steak and Potatoes – Hot or Cold

1 pound small red potatoes
3 cups broccoli florets, steamed
(green beans or asparagus may be substituted for broccoli)
1 small red onion, thickly-sliced
1 red bell pepper, cut into bite-sized chunks
1 pound beef top sirloin steak, grilled
2 tablespoons apple cider vinegar
¼ cup olive oil
2 garlic cloves, minced
½ teaspoon ground mustard
¼ teaspoon salt
¼ teaspoon black pepper
½ teaspoon paprika

Cut potatoes into wedges. Place in a large saucepan; cover with water. Bring to a boil; lower heat to medium and cook 10-15 minutes or until potatoes are fork-tender. Remove from heat; drain.

Slice cooked steak, across the grain, into thin slices; set aside.

In a large bowl, place potatoes, cooked broccoli, red onion, and red pepper. Pour dressing over all; toss to coat. Add steak slices; toss gently to coat.

To serve hot, grill steaks while potatoes cook.

To serve cold or at room temperature, using left-over steak is a timesaver.

To make Vinaigrette:
In a small jar, combine vinegar, oil, garlic, mustard, salt, black pepper, and paprika; cover tightly and shake well.

Serve this dish with crusty bread and a salad, per Jennifer Eve. "This is a recipe that I have just been winging for years," she says, "so exact measurements are a challenge, but here goes. Make homemade broth. You can buy it in a can, but it is so much better to make it yourself. Here's what I do."

Chicken and Wild Rice Soup

Buy a whole chicken. Rinse it out, then put it in a large stockpot with plenty of water to cover and then some. I add one quartered onion (don't bother to peel it,) a handful of baby carrots (or two regular-sized ones, just break them up,) 3 stalks of celery, broken in a few pieces, some peppercorns (probably about 10,) two bay leaves, and a little salt. Let the chicken come to a boil, then let it simmer for about an hour. Remove the chicken and let it cool.

Strain the broth through a colander and return the liquid to the stockpot. De-bone the chicken, tearing it into bite-sized pieces.

(Or, substitute canned broth and cooked chicken.)

Heat the broth to boiling, then reduce heat to simmer and add:
1 cup diced carrots
3 stalks celery, diced
1 onion, diced
1 bay leaf
1 tablespoon curry powder
1 tablespoon powdered thyme
    (or 4 fresh thyme stalks, destemmed. Add leaves to pot.)
1 tablespoon salt
1 tablespoon black pepper
1 cup uncooked wild rice
1 can cream of mushroom soup
1 can cream of chicken soup

Simmer until the rice is done, usually 30-45 minutes. Add chicken; heat through.

Vegetarian Meatballs

1 cup dry lentils
2 large eggs
2/3 cup Italian-flavored breadcrumbs
1/3 cup ricotta cheese
¼ cup grated Parmesan cheese
1 tablespoon chopped fresh parsley
Salt and pepper
Marinara sauce
Olive oil

Cook lentils in water until tender, about 20 minutes. Yield should be about 2 cups. Drain and cool 10 minutes.

In a food processor, pulse cooked lentils until finely chopped.

In a mixing bowl, combine lentils, eggs, breadcrumbs, cheeses, parsley, salt, and pepper. Mix by hand until blended. Cover bowl and refrigerate at least 2 hours.

Shape the mixture into 1½ inch balls. Yield: 15 meatballs.

In a saucepan, bring marinara sauce to a simmer.

Coat the bottom of a large skillet with olive oil and place over medium-high heat. Cook meatballs 7-8 minutes, or until golden brown on all sides.

Transfer cooked meatballs to sauce; slow simmer 30-40 minutes.

Serve alone or over a bed of pasta or rice.

Note: With texture and flavor similar to ground beef meatballs, these can be served without sauce, but the sauce enhances their flavor.

One serving of lentils, without changing any other items of your diet, is reported to reduce cholesterol levels by fifty points.

Spicy Pulled Pork Sandwiches

1 (2½ -pound) boneless pork shoulder
Salt
Black pepper
1 large onion, cut into wedges
1 (18-ounce) bottle spicy barbecue sauce
1 cup Dr. Pepper, non-diet
8 hamburger buns
Pickles (dill, sour, bread-and-butter, and sweet)
1 large onion, sliced in rounds

Trim excess fat from pork. Sprinkle meat with salt and pepper.

Place onion in bottom of slow cooker. Place meat on top of onion, cutting to fit inside slow cooker if necessary.

Stir barbecue sauce and soft drink together; pour mixture over meat. Cover and cook on low setting for 8-10 hours.

When tender, transfer meat to a cutting board and onion to a large bowl. Shred meat, using two forks. Add meat to onion in bowl

Skim fat from liquid in slow cooker. Add enough liquid to bowl to keep meat moistened.

Prepare a small serving tray with onion slices and an assortment of pickles.

Using a large slotted spoon, serve meat mixture on buns. Serve with pickle tray and lots of napkins.

Quick-Fix Lemon Chicken

½ cup flour
1 tablespoon Italian seasoning
1 teaspoon dried parsley
½ teaspoon salt
1 pound chicken cutlets
2 tablespoons vegetable oil
1 cup chicken broth
1 tablespoon lemon juice

In a small bowl, mix together flour, seasoning, parsley, and salt. Reserve 1 tablespoon for sauce and set it aside. Place remaining flour mixture in a large plastic bag with a zipper seal. Sprinkle chicken cutlets lightly with water and shake, one cutlet at a time, in flour. Set cutlets on a rack after shaking.

Heat oil in a large nonstick skillet over medium heat. Add chicken, but do not crowd. Cook 3 minutes per side or until golden brown. Remove from skillet and keep warm. Cook remaining cutlets, adding more oil if required. Remove final cutlets from skillet.

Mix broth and lemon juice to reserved tablespoon of flour mixture. Add to skillet and bring to a boil, releasing fond from pan. Stir frequently while cooking 5 minutes, or until slightly thickened.

To serve, spoon sauce over chicken.

Shrimp and Snow Peas

12 ounces frozen shrimp, thawed
8 ounces snow peas
1 tablespoon olive oil
3 cloves garlic, minced
1 teaspoon grated ginger
¼ teaspoon cayenne
¾ cup unsweetened coconut milk
½ teaspoon salt
¼ teaspoon lime zest
Cooked rice or angel hair pasta
2 tablespoons finely-chopped celery
Lime slices

Rinse shrimp and pat dry with paper towels; set aside. Remove tips and strings from snow peas; set aside.

Heat oil in a large skillet over medium-high heat. Add snow pea pods and cook 2-3 minutes, stirring until peas are crisp tender. Remove from skillet; set aside.

Combine shrimp, garlic, ginger, and cayenne in skillet; cook and stir until shrimp turn opaque but not pink, about 2 minutes. Add coconut milk, salt, and lime zest; cook until heated through. Return peas to skillet to reheat.

Serve shrimp over heated rice or a thin bed of angel hair pasta. Garnish with celery and lime slices.

Shepherd's Pie should be a staple in the Shepherd household, but I seldom make it. This is a great alternative.

Shepherd's Pie in a Potato

6 large baking potatoes
2 tablespoons olive oil
1 pound ground beef
1 yellow onion, chopped
1 green bell pepper, chopped
1 red bell pepper, chopped
1 cup frozen green peas, thawed
½ cup frozen whole kernel corn, thawed
2 tablespoons ketchup
3 tablespoons Worcestershire sauce
1 teaspoon garlic powder
1 teaspoon onion powder
1 ½ teaspoons paprika
¼ teaspoon cayenne
¼ teaspoon salt
¼ teaspoon black pepper
1 can cut green beans
1 stick butter or margarine
¾ cup whipping cream
¼ cup milk
1 cup grated Colby cheese
1 cup grated Monterey Jack cheese

Preheat oven to 375°.

Wash and dry potatoes; cut several slits in each one; rub with oil and wrap each in aluminum foil and place on a baking sheet. Bake 1 hour, or until done. Remove from oven to cool slightly.

In a large skillet, brown beef with onion and bell peppers; drain away grease. Add peas, corn, ketchup, Worcestershire sauce, garlic and onion powders, paprika, cayenne, salt, and black pepper. Cook and stir until peas and corn are tender. Add green beans; cook until warmed through; remove skillet from heat; set aside.

Unwrap potatoes; keep potatoes on baking sheet. With a sharp knife, slice off a thin top of each potato; snack on slices. With large spoon, scoop cooked potato from its peel, leaving a thin shell; set aside.

In a bowl, mash potato pulp with butter, cream, milk, and half of the cheeses until combined.

With a spoon, pack 1 cup beef mixture into each potato shell; cover with ½ cup potato mixture. Bake 15-20 minutes.

Top potatoes with remaining ½ cup of Colby and Monterey Jack cheeses. Bake until cheese melts, about 5 minutes. Remove from oven; let cool slightly before serving.

Frankfurter Crown Casserole

2 slices bacon
½ cup onion, chopped fine
1 can cream of mushroom soup
½ cup water
½ teaspoon salt
1/8 teaspoon black pepper
3 cups boiled red potatoes, peeled and sliced into thin rounds
1 cup cooked green beans
½ pound frankfurters, split lengthwise and cut in half

Preheat oven to 350°.

Cook bacon in skillet; remove and crumble bacon; set aside. Cook onion in bacon drippings. Stir in soup, water, salt and pepper; add potatoes and green beans. Pour mixture into a 1½-quart casserole dish; stand up frankfurters around edge. Bake for 30 minutes; remove from oven and garnish with bacon.

Frank Stew

1 pound ground beef
4 frankfurters, sliced in 1-inch pieces
2 (16-ounce) cans baked beans
½ cup barbecue sauce
Shredded cheddar cheese
Chopped onion
Hot sauce

In a large saucepan, brown beef; drain off grease and discard it. Add frankfurters, baked beans, and barbecue sauce to beef; stir to combine; bring mixture to a boil. Reduce heat; cover pan and simmer 6-8 minutes.

Serve hot stew in bowls with shredded cheese, onion, and hot sauce on the side.

Harvest Ham

1 ham steak, 2 inches thick
2 cups sweet cider
½ cup brown sugar, packed
½ cup cranberries, chopped fine
½ cup seedless raisins
2 whole cloves
Rind of 1 orange, grated
Juice of 1 orange

Preheat oven to 325°.

Place ham steak in a shallow baking pan.

In a small bowl, combine cider, brown sugar, cranberries, raisins, cloves, orange rind and juice; mix well. Pour mixture over ham steak.

Bake, basting frequently, for 30 minutes per pound of meat. Add more cider, if needed. Remove ham steak to platter when done.

Serve hot.

If you like sauce or gravy, thicken pan juices with 1 tablespoon flour to 1 cup juice. Simmer until desired consistency.

The two fishes most used in casseroles: salmon and tuna. You can buy mixes, but why not make casseroles from scratch? They're quick and easy, and you usually have all of the ingredients in your pantry.

Salmon Casserole

1 can condensed cream of celery soup
¼ cup milk
½ cup mayonnaise (Miracle Whip Salad Dressing preferred)
1 (16-ounce) can salmon, drained and flaked
1 tablespoon onion, chopped
1 (10-ounce) package frozen peas, cooked
2 cups cooked noodles
Butter

Preheat oven to 350°. Butter a 1½-quart casserole dish. Combine soup, milk and mayonnaise in a large bowl; blend well. Add salmon, onion, peas and noodles; toss until coated. Pour into the casserole dish and bake for 25 minutes.

Variations:
1. Canned tuna may be substituted for the salmon for a **Tuna Casserole**.
2. Cream of potato soup or cream of mushroom soup may be substituted for the cream of celery soup.
3. If you like cheese, add ¼ cup grated parmesan cheese to the mixture before cooking and/or top the casserole with ½ cup shredded cheddar cheese for the last 5 minutes of baking.

Meatloaf

1 large egg
1 teaspoon salt
½ teaspoon black pepper
1 tablespoon dried parsley
1 pound ground beef
1 small yellow onion, chopped
½ cup green bell pepper, chopped (optional)
1 (8-ounce) can tomato sauce
½ cup crushed saltine crackers
Ketchup

Preheat oven to 350°.

In a large bowl, beat egg with a fork. Add salt, black pepper, parsley, ground beef, onion, and bell pepper. Mix well, using your hand. Add tomato sauce and crushed crackers; mix well. Add more crackers, if needed, to make mixture hold together.

Place meatloaf mixture in a 9-inch loaf pan or shape it into a loaf on a rimmed baking sheet. Decorate top of meatloaf with a heavy drizzle of ketchup.

Bake for 1 hour, until well browned and a knife comes out clean when inserted into the middle of the loaf. Slice and serve hot.

Variations: Instead of ketchup, cover top with barbecue sauce. Or, combine 1 tablespoon mustard, 1/3 cup ketchup, and 2 tablespoons light brown sugar to spread on top of meatloaf before baking.

Note: Slice leftover meatloaf for sandwiches. Almost everyone loves a cold meatloaf sandwich. But, I prefer it warm, so I reheat meatloaf slices in the microwave and make a sandwich on fresh white bread with cold mayonnaise.

Layered Meatloaf

1 pound ground beef
1 pound ground pork
1 cup onion, chopped fine
1 clove garlic, minced
2 large eggs
1/3 cup milk
1 cup fresh bread crumbs
1 teaspoon salt
½ teaspoon black pepper
6 ounces roasted red peppers, drained well
1 (10-ounce) box frozen spinach, thawed and squeezed dry
1 (8-ounce) can tomato sauce
½ teaspoon Italian seasoning

Heat oven to 350°.
Have ready a foil-lined, rimmed baking sheet.
In a large bowl, mix beef, pork, onion, garlic, eggs, milk, bread crumbs, salt, and black pepper. Divide in thirds. Shape each portion into a 9x5-inch bar. Place one bar in the center of baking sheet.
Dry red peppers with paper towels. Cover top of bar with peppers. Lay another meat bar on top of peppers.
Squeeze spinach dry and cover top of second bar with spinach. Add remaining meat bar. Mix tomato sauce with seasoning and spread on top of bar.
Bake meatloaf, uncovered, for 1 hour. Remove from oven and let stand for 10 minutes before serving. (A serrated knife makes for easy slicing.)

3-Bean Hot Dish

¼ pound bacon
1 pound ground beef
¼ cup onion, chopped
¼ cup ketchup
½ cup brown sugar
1 can lima beans
1 can kidney beans
1 can oven-baked beans
2 teaspoons prepared mustard

Preheat oven to 350°. Butter a large casserole dish.

Brown bacon, ground beef and onion in skillet; drain on paper towels. Combine meat mixture with remaining ingredients in large bowl, mix lightly. Pour into casserole dish and bake for one hour. Serve hot.

Smoked Brisket Indoors

1 (4-5-pound) beef brisket
2 teaspoons meat tenderizer
½ teaspoon celery salt
½ teaspoon seasoned salt
½ teaspoon garlic salt
¼ cup liquid smoke
¼ cup Worcestershire sauce
Barbecue sauce

Place brisket on a sheet of aluminum foil, large enough to wrap it tightly. Sprinkle meat tenderizer and salts on both sides of meat. Pour liquid smoke and Worcestershire sauce over top of meat. Seal brisket in aluminum foil; place in a large pan in the refrigerator. Marinate 6 hours or overnight.

Remove brisket from pan; keep wrapped in foil. Place meat in slow cooker. Set slow cooker to low and cook 8-10 hours. Remove from slow cooker; let cool. When cool, place in refrigerator to chill.

When ready to serve, remove foil from meat. Slice the chilled brisket into thin slices, reheat, and pour barbeque sauce over meat.

Barbecue Sauce

½ cup dark brown sugar, packed
½ cup minced onion
4 tablespoons tomato paste
2 cups ketchup
½ cup apple cider vinegar
3 tablespoons Worcestershire sauce
4 teaspoons liquid smoke
¼ teaspoon hot pepper sauce
1 ½ teaspoons salt
½ teaspoon black pepper

Combine all ingredients in a saucepan; stir and bring to a boil. Reduce to low; simmer 20 minutes. Strain and serve.

Beef Cubes in Sour Cream

2 pounds beef shank, cut in 1-inch cubes
2 medium onions, sliced
½ cup dairy sour cream
½ cup water
2 tablespoons American cheese, grated
Salt and Pepper
Vegetable Shortening

Roll meat in flour; brown in shortening in a hot skillet. Add onion; cook a few more minutes. Combine sour cream, water, cheese, salt and pepper in a small bowl; pour mixture over meat; reduce heat to a low simmer. Cover pan tightly and cook slowly until tender, about 2 hours.

Halibut Steaks with Corn Salad

1 tablespoon olive oil
Pinch of red pepper flakes
4 small halibut steaks
3-4 tablespoons butter

In a large nonstick skillet, heat olive oil; add red pepper flakes; let sizzle for 30 seconds.

Dry halibut steaks with paper towels. Place in skillet and cook 2½ minutes. Turn steaks over to cook another 2½ minutes. During second cooking time, add butter to skillet. Spoon melted butter over steaks, continuously basting until steaks are done. Remove steaks from skillet.

Serve with corn salad.

Corn Salad

3 tomatoes, coarsely chopped
1 red onion, sliced thin
1 tablespoon dried parsley
1 tablespoon minced cilantro
¼ cup balsamic vinegar
1 teaspoon salt
½ teaspoon black pepper
4 cups fresh (or frozen) corn kernels
1 tablespoon olive oil
1 tablespoon butter
1 tablespoon Dijon mustard
1 scallion, chopped

In a large bowl, combine tomatoes, onion, parsley, cilantro, vinegar, salt, and pepper; set aside.

In a saute pan, cook corn with oil and butter until tender. Remove from heat; stir in mustard; add corn to bowl of salad, tossing to coat. Garnish with scallion.

Sweet & Sour Chicken

1 pound boneless chicken breasts
½ teaspoon salt
½ teaspoon garlic powder
½ teaspoon ground ginger
1 tablespoon soy sauce
1 tablespoon chicken broth
1 (20-ounce) can unsweetened pineapple chunks
2 tablespoons cornstarch
2 tablespoons granulated sugar
¼ cup apple cider vinegar
¼ cup ketchup
2 teaspoons soy sauce
1/3 cup cornstarch
1 tablespoon vegetable oil
Cooked rice
1 green onion, sliced in thin rings

Remove skin from chicken; cut chicken breasts into 1-inch pieces; place in a large plastic bag. In a small bowl, combine salt, garlic, ginger, tablespoon of soy sauce; and broth; stir until blended. Pour mixture over chicken and seal bag. Massage until chicken pieces are coated. Place bag in a bowl in refrigerator to marinate 30 minutes.

Drain pineapple, reserving juice; set pineapple aside. Measure juice, adding water if needed, to make 1 cup. In a small jar with lid, combine 2 tablespoons cornstarch and sugar. Add pineapple juice, vinegar, ketchup, and 2 teaspoons soy sauce. Cover and shake until mixed; set aside.

Remove chicken from refrigerator; drain and discard marinade. Place 1/3 cup cornstarch in new plastic bag. Add chicken pieces, in several batches; shake to coat. In a large, nonstick skillet, heat oil and stir-fry chicken until done; remove from skillet. Add pineapple juice mixture to skillet; bring to a boil, stirring until thickened, for about 2 minutes. Add pineapple chunks and return chicken pieces to pan; heat through.

Serve over a bed of hot rice. Garnish with green onion.

Ham Jambalaya

1/3 cup butter
½ cup chopped green onion
½ cup chopped white onion
1 large green pepper, cut in strips
½ cup chopped celery
1 teaspoon minced garlic
1 pound raw shrimp, peeled
1 (16-ounce) can tomatoes
1 cup chicken broth
½ teaspoon salt
¼ teaspoon cayenne
1 cup raw rice
1 cup cooked ham, cubed

In a large pan, melt butter. Add onions, green pepper, celery, and garlic; saute until tender but not browned. Add shrimp; cook 5 minutes. Add tomatoes, broth, salt, cayenne, uncooked rice, and ham; stir. Cover and cook 25-30 minutes over low heat or until rice is cooked through. Tomato juice may be added if mixture seems dry.

Chicken Roma

2 (8-ounce) cans tomato sauce
1 teaspoon Italian seasoning
½ teaspoon garlic powder
½ teaspoon onion powder
1 teaspoon dried parsley flakes
1 pound boneless skinless chicken breasts
¾ cup bread crumbs
2 teaspoons dried oregano
¼ teaspoon salt
2 eggs
2 tablespoons water
½ cup flour
¼ cup vegetable or olive oil
1 cup shredded mozzarella cheese
¼ cup shredded Parmesan cheese
Angel hair pasta

Have handy three pie plates or shallow bowls.

In a small saucepan, combine tomato sauce, Italian seasoning, garlic and onion powders, and parsley flakes; heat and keep warm.

Trim and pound chicken breasts, if needed, to flatten each to a ¼-inch thickness; set aside.

In one bowl, combine bread crumbs, oregano, and salt. In second bowl, beat eggs and water with a fork. Place flour in third bowl. Coat chicken breasts, one at a time, with flour, patting away excess; dip in egg bowl, and then press in crumb mixture.

Heat oil in a large skillet; cook coated chicken breasts 4-6 minutes on each side; remove from heat; keep warm.

Cook angel hair pasta in salted water, drain.

For serving, arrange pasta on four plates. Place a chicken breast on top of pasta, and spoon sauce over center of chicken, instead of covering all the crunchy coating. Serve remainder of sauce at the table in a gravy boat.

Rosemary Pork Loin

3 cloves garlic
1 tablespoon dried rosemary
1 teaspoon salt
½ teaspoon black pepper
1 (2-pound) boneless pork loin roast
½ cup olive oil
½ cup white wine

Preheat oven to 350°.

Crush garlic with rosemary, salt and pepper, to make a paste. Place meat in a roasting pan. Pierce meat with a sharp knife in several places and press the garlic paste into the openings. Mix olive oil with any remaining garlic paste; rub on meat.

Bake pork loin in oven, turning and basting with pan liquids twice. Cook until the pork is no longer pink in the center and registers 145° on a thermometer. Remove roast to a platter.

Heat the wine in the roasting pan and stir to loosen browned bits of food from bottom of pan.

Slice pork and serve with pan juices.

Roast Pork with Pear Chutney

1 cup water
1 (4 to 6-pound) boneless pork loin roast
1 teaspoon salt
1 teaspoon black pepper

Preheat oven to 400°.

Place water and meat in a large roasting pan, fat side up. Pierce meat with a sharp knife in several places. Sprinkle with salt and pepper.

Bake pork loin, uncovered, in oven for 45 minutes. Reduce heat to 250°. Baste with juices. Cover and bake 2-3 hours until pork loin is tender; baste with juices. Remove roast to a platter. Tent with aluminum foil; let rest for 10 minutes.

Slice roast and serve with chutney.

Pear Chutney

3 pears
2 tablespoons butter
½ apple cider vinegar
½ cup sugar
½ cup golden raisins
1 teaspoon ground ginger
¼ teaspoon ground cayenne
½ teaspoon allspice
½ teaspoon paprika

Peel and core pears; cut into 1-inch pieces.

In a saucepan, melt butter and saute pears for 2 minutes. Add all of the remaining ingredients; stir and bring to a boil. Lower heat and stir occasionally while cooking mixture until thickened, about 45 minutes. Remove from heat. Spoon over roast pork.

Turkey Chow Mein

3 cups roasted turkey, cubed
½ cup cashews, whole or halved
½ cup onion, chopped fine
3 cups celery, chopped
1 cup water or chicken broth
2 cans cream of chicken soup
Salt and Pepper, to taste
1 large can chow mein noodles

Preheat oven to 350°. Butter a large casserole dish.

Mix broth and soup in large bowl; add turkey, cashews, onion, celery, salt, and pepper. Pour into casserole dish and bake for 25-30 minutes. Remove from heat and serve turkey mixture over a bed of chow mein noodles.

Tater Tot Casserole

1 pound ground beef
½ white onion, chopped
Salt and pepper
1 package frozen tater tots
1 can cheddar cheese soup

Preheat oven to 350°.

Brown hamburger and onion in a skillet; add salt and pepper to taste. Spread meat mixture in a casserole dish. Place frozen potatoes evenly over meat. Pour soup over all.

Place casserole in oven and bake for one hour.

Hamburger and Rice Casserole

2 pounds ground beef
2 onions, chopped
1 cup celery, chopped
1 can cream of mushroom soup
1 can cream of chicken soup
2 cups rice
2-3 cups water
Soy sauce

Preheat oven to 350°.

Lightly brown ground beef in a heavy stockpot or Dutch oven; drain grease. Add onions, celery, soups, rice, and 2 cups water to meat; mix well. Cover pot and bake for 2 hours; adding more water as needed.

Serve with soy sauce. Serves 12.

One-Pan Spaghetti Dinner

1 tablespoon shortening or olive oil
1 pound ground beef
¾ cup chopped onion
½ cup chopped green pepper
1 clove garlic, minced
2 teaspoons salt
4 cups water
½ pound spaghetti, broken into 2-inch pieces
1 (16-ounce) can tomatoes
¾ cup ketchup
Tossed salad
Breadsticks

In a large saucepan, melt shortening. Add ground beef, onion, and green pepper; saute until meat is brown. Add garlic and saute another minute. Sprinkle mixture with salt. Stir in water. Bring mixture to a boil. Stir in spaghetti.

Cook over medium heat, uncovered, 12-15 minutes, or until spaghetti is tender. Stir in tomatoes and ketchup; cover and simmer 8-10 minutes for flavors to blend.

Serves 6-8.

Serve spaghetti entre beside a green tossed salad and heated breadsticks.

Chili

½ cup onion, diced
2 tablespoons green bell pepper, diced
2 tablespoons salad oil
½ pound ground beef
½ cup boiling water
1 cup canned tomatoes, crushed
1 tablespoons cold water
1½ tablespoons chili powder
¼ teaspoon salt
1 teaspoon sugar
1½ teaspoons minced garlic
2 cups cooked kidney beans

Cook onion and green pepper in salad oil in skillet until tender; add beef and cook uncovered until browned. Add boiling water and tomatoes. In small bowl, mix cold water and chili powder into a smooth paste; add to meat mixture with salt, sugar and minced garlic. Cover skillet and simmer 1 hour; uncover and simmer ½ hour or until meat is tender. Add beans and heat through. If chili is too thick, add 1 cup water or tomato juice.

This has been one of my most-requested meat recipes for some years. I love potatoes and add extra when making it for myself. The stew is good warmed over and makes a great lunch at the office.

Beef Stew with an Italian Kick

2 pounds lean beef, cut into 1-inch cubes
Flour and vegetable shortening
4 large carrots, peeled and sliced in ½-inch rounds
4 large red potatoes, peeled and chopped into bite-sized pieces
1 large yellow onion, peeled and chopped into bite-sized pieces
1½ cans beef broth
1 can tomato soup
1 teaspoon salt
½ teaspoon black pepper
1 teaspoon Italian seasoning
1½ teaspoon parsley flakes
2 (8-ounce) cans tomato sauce
½ cup water

Dust beef cubes with flour and brown in shortening in hot skillet. Remove from heat and set aside. Pour half of beef broth into bottom of slow cooker. Single-layer carrots, potatoes and beef in slow cooker and top with onions. In 4-cup measure or small mixing bowl, combine tomato soup, salt, pepper, Italian seasoning and parsley flakes; mix well with a fork or small whisk. Stir in tomato sauce, water and remaining beef broth. Pour over items in slow cooker. Cover and cook on High setting for 1 hour; stir mixture and switch to Low setting. After about 6 hours, or when vegetables are tender, remove cover and let set until stew is cool enough to eat.

Serving suggestion: To complement the stew's hearty taste, serve with thick tortilla chips Deep-frying them yourself is best.

Yes, this is stew plus soup but not connected with a popular television personality's stewp. I've made stoup probably before she started cooking. She's brilliant, by the way.

My stoup is made from leftover stew and, with new ingredients, becomes a different type of dish so it doesn't fit into the "leftovers" category. Besides, it makes the meal stretch. No can resist saving money. See what you can do to change your leftovers.

Barbara's Stoup

½ recipe of left-over **Beef Stew with an Italian Kick**
1 cup frozen green peas, cooked and drained
1 cup tomato juice
2 tablespoons ketchup
1½ cups macaroni, cooked to al dente
Salt and Pepper, to taste

Pour beef stew into large saucepan and cut tender beef and vegetables into smaller pieces with a large spoon. Add peas, juice, ketchup, and macaroni; cook until heated through. Remove from heat; taste, and add salt and pepper, if needed. Serve warm, with crackers on the side.

Getting up before dawn on the farm meant being greeted by the aroma of fresh-cooked bacon or sausage and hearing the sizzle of eggs frying in a skillet. Yum! Breakfast Casserole is a great substitute. Prepare it the night before and it will be ready to pop into the oven the next morning, baking while you get ready for work.

Breakfast Casserole

1 pound ground sausage
8 eggs, beaten
6 slices white bread, cut into cubes
2 cups whole milk
1 teaspoon dry mustard
1 teaspoon salt
1 cup cheddar cheese, shredded

Spray 9"x13" baking pan with cooking spray.

Brown sausage in skillet; remove and drain on paper towels; set aside. In large mixing bowl, combine eggs, bread cubes, milk, mustard, salt, and cheese; stir in sausage. Pour mixture into baking pan; refrigerate overnight.

The next morning, remove pan from refrigerator and preheat oven to 350°. Bake casserole 40-50 minutes. Remove from oven; slice and serve hot.

Serving Suggestion:

Serve casserole for dinner or on a breakfast buffet with **Frozen Cranberry Salad**. The recipe is in this book in the Salads section.

Country-Style Roast Beef with Gravy

1 (4-5 pound) eye of round, or rump, roast
1 tablespoon shortening
Water
2 onions, quartered
3-4 russet baking potatoes, cut into chunks
3-4 carrots, sliced thick
Salt
Pepper
Cornstarch

Preheat oven to 325°.

Have available a large roasting pan.

With a knife, trim excess fat from roast. Melt shortening in skillet and add roast. Brown roast slowly in skillet until all sides are browned. Transfer roast to roasting pan.

Add 3 cups water to skillet; loosen drippings; pour into roast pan. Place in oven. Cook, uncovered, until all liquid, except grease, has evaporated. A dark brown residue will be visible where liquid was. To this, add 4-5 cups water and stir, scraping bottom of roasting pan. Continue to cook another 2 hours or so.

Add onions, potatoes, carrots, salt, and pepper to roasting pan. If liquid in pan is insufficient to almost cover vegetables, add more water. As vegetables cook, occasionally spoon drippings over. When vegetables are tender, remove them and roast beef from pan; place where they will stay warm while you make gravy.

Roast Gravy

In a small cup, stir 3-4 tablespoons cornstarch in ½ cup water until well blended; pour into roasting pan to thicken meat drippings. Stir drippings rapidly so that gravy will be smooth.

Put roasting pan in oven; cook a minute or two, until gravy is transparent. Gravy should be rich, dark brown, and rather thick. Add more salt, if needed.

Serve gravy with roast and vegetables.

Vegetables & Sides

Chili Cheese Hand Warmers

Bake as many potatoes as you wish; whatever size you wish. Wash the potatoes and pierce skins; bake in a 400° F oven until fork-tender (Time will depend on potato size.) Cut a ½-inch slice from the small end of each potato, or halve potatoes. Carefully scoop out pulp, leaving skins intact. Coarsely mash pulp with a fork. For each cup of potato pulp, mix:

- 2 tablespoons milk
- 2 tablespoons canned diced green chiles
- 1½ tablespoons diced green onion
- ¼ cup shredded Monterey Jack or cheddar cheese
- salt to taste

Pack into potato shells, mounding tops slightly. Place on a cookie sheet and bake at 400° F until heated through. Wrap each potato in a napkin to eat out of hand.

Squash Ribbons

2 medium-size zucchini
2 medium-size yellow squash
4 slices bacon, fried crisp and crumbled
2 tablespoons butter or bacon grease
½ cup onion, diced
½ teaspoon black pepper
4 ounces Parmesan cheese

Wash zucchini and yellow squash; pat dry; cut off ends; do not peel colored skins. With a vegetable peeler, slice down the length of each squash to make long, thin ribbons. Turn each squash to slice down all four sides. Continue slicing until the seeds surface. Discard center (seedy) sections of vegetables. Set ribbons aside.

With cheese slicer or vegetable peeler, slice thin ribbons from block of cheese; set aside.

In a large skillet over medium heat, melt butter or grease. Saute onion until almost tender. Place squash ribbons on top of onion and cook, turning squash a time or two with tongs, until tender but not mushy – takes only a couple of minutes. Remove from heat.

With tongs, transfer ribbons to a large serving dish, sprinkle with pepper and add half the cheese. Toss lightly. Top with remaining cheese and bacon.

Serve immediately.

Peppered Bacon and Sprouts

4 slices peppered bacon, thick-sliced
½ cup onion, sliced
2 pounds Brussels sprouts
½ teaspoon salt
¼ teaspoon cracked black pepper
¾ cup chicken broth
¾ cup evaporated milk

Clean sprouts; peeling away an outer leaf of each bulb. Slice sprouts in half, pole to pole. Set aside.

In a large skillet over medium heat, cook bacon until crisp. Remove from skillet; let drain on wire rack or paper towels. Reserve 2 tablespoons in skillet of bacon drippings. Add sprouts and cook for 4 minutes, turning sprouts a couple of times. Sprinkle with salt and pepper. Add chicken broth and heat to boiling. Reduce heat and simmer, covered, for 5 minutes. Then, uncover it and cook 2-4 minutes, or until bottom of skillet is almost dry. Pour in cream and stir gently. Cook until sauce is thickened, about 4 more minutes.

Transfer sprouts to a warmed serving platter. Tear bacon into large pieces. Top sprouts with bacon and serve.

When you need a quick and easy side dish for unexpected company, or when you're just too busy to peel and mash potatoes, etc., try this recipe. Use it as a springboard for your own creation. You could add a can of Veg-All®, drained and its liquid discarded, for a good way to get toddlers to eat their vegetables.

Noodles and Peas

1 (14-ounce) can beef broth
2 ounces water
2 cups wide egg noodles
1 cup frozen green peas
Salt and Pepper

Pour broth and water into medium-sized saucepan, bring to a boil. Add noodles and stir in peas; bring mixture back to a boil. Reduce heat to a simmer; cover and cook about 10 minutes, or until noodles are cooked and peas are tender. Add salt and pepper to meet your taste preference. Do not drain broth. Serve warm.

Variation 1: For **Beef Noodles and Peas**, prepare Noodles and Peas recipe, adding ½ to 1 cup thinly-sliced cooked beef to the mixture. Cover and simmer just until beef is heated through. Do not drain broth. Serve warm. (A great way to incorporate left-over roast beef or brisket.)

Variation 2: For **Chicken Noodles and Peas**, prepare Noodles and Peas recipe, substituting chicken broth for the beef broth and adding ½ to 1 cup shredded cooked chicken to the mixture. Cover and simmer just until chicken is heated through. Do not drain broth. Serve warm. (A great way to incorporate left-over rotisserie or baked chicken.)

Potatoes with Chives

6 medium potatoes
1 (8-ounce) package cream cheese, softened
½ cup evaporated milk
1 tablespoon snipped chives
1½ teaspoon lemon juice
¼ cup butter, softened
½ teaspoon garlic salt
Dash of black pepper
Long chives, for garnish

Heat oven to 350°.
Have ready a buttered casserole dish.
Wash and peel potatoes; cut into chunks. Cook in a saucepan of boiling salted water until tender. Drain water from pan; shake over flame to dry potatoes. Mash potatoes in pan. Add ¼ cup milk, the butter, garlic salt, and pepper. Blend and set aside.
In a small bowl, combine cream cheese, remaining ¼ cup of the milk, the chives, and lemon juice. Add this mixture to potatoes; stir until blended. Spoon into casserole dish
Cover with foil and bake until heated through.
Uncover and garnish with additional chives.

Green Bean Casserole

1 (10¾-ounce) can cream of mushroom soup
¾ cup milk
1/8 teaspoon black pepper
1 teaspoon soy sauce (optional)
2 cans (4 cups) green beans
1 can (1 1/3 cups) French-fried onions

Preheat oven to 350°.

In a 1½–quart baking dish, mix soup, milk, pepper, and soy sauce, if desired. Stir in beans and 2/3 cup onions.

Bake for 25 minutes. Stir.

Top mixture with remaining 2/3 cup onions; bake an additional 5 minutes.

Remove from oven and serve.

Note: Cut green beans work better than French-style sliced beans in this recipe. Since this dish is practically a requirement in most homes at holiday time, make extra. Also, this is a great dish for novice cooks to prepare and bring to a potluck dinner any time of the year. It's easy to prepare, has few ingredients, and not much measuring.

Broccoli-Rice Casserole

2 boxes frozen broccoli, thawed
1 cup Minute® Rice
2 tablespoons butter
1 tablespoon onion flakes
1 can cream of chicken soup
1 can milk (soup can measure)
½ cup Cheese Whiz®
¾ cup fresh bread crumbs
½ cup grated parmesan cheese
Butter (for pan)

Preheat oven to 300°. Butter bottom of casserole pan.

In a bowl, mix broccoli, rice, butter, onion flakes, soup, milk, and Cheese Whiz®. Pour into prepared pan.

Combine bread crumbs and parmesan cheese; spread this over broccoli mixture.

Bake 1 hour.

Cabbage and Bacon

2 slices bacon
1 onion, thinly-sliced
1 red bell pepper, sliced into thin strips
4 cups shredded green cabbage
2 tablespoons water
2 tablespoons mayonnaise
1 tablespoon ground mustard
1 tablespoon apple cider vinegar
¼ teaspoon celery seeds

Chop bacon into 1-inch pieces; cook in a nonstick skillet over medium heat until crispy. Remove bacon from pan; set aside.

Combine onion, bell pepper, cabbage, and water in same skillet; cover and cook 5 minutes, stirring a few times, until vegetables are crisp tender.

Combine mayonnaise, mustard, vinegar, and celery seeds in a small bowl; add to skillet. Toss to coat cabbage mixture with dressing. Remove from heat.

Serve warm, garnished with crispy bacon.

Sesame Green Beans and Snow Peas

1½ teaspoons sesame oil
1 tablespoon canola oil
1 pound fresh green beans
½ pound snow peas
1 tablespoon soy sauce
2 tablespoons toasted sesame seeds

Wash and string green beans and snow peas; keep whole. Set aside.

Heat sesame oil and canola oil in a large skillet over medium heat. When oil is hot, add green beans. Cook and stir, uncovered, until beans turn bright green. Add snow peas; continue to cook until green beans start to brown – about 10 minutes total cooking time. Remove from heat.

Stir in soy sauce. Cover skillet; let stand 5 minutes.

Uncover and spoon beans and peas onto serving plate. Sprinkle with sesame seeds.

Mixed Potato Wedges

3 russet baking potatoes
3 sweet potatoes
Cooking spray
1 tablespoon olive oil
1 teaspoon caraway seeds
¼ teaspoon garlic powder
1 teaspoon dried thyme

Preheat oven to 425°.

Have ready a baking sheet made nonstick with cooking spray.

Wash and scrub potatoes; do not peel. Cut into quarters, horizontally.

In a large bowl, combine olive oil and spices. Add potato wedges; mix until well coated. Put potatoes in a single layer on baking sheet.

Bake until tender. (Time varies, depending on size of potatoes.)

Italian Zucchini

4 zucchini squash, unpeeled and sliced
4 tablespoons butter
½ cup chopped onion
½ cup chopped green bell pepper
1 (3-ounce) can sliced mushrooms
1 package spaghetti sauce mix
1 cup water
1 (6-ounce) can tomato paste
1 (4-ounce) package mozzarella cheese, shredded
2 tablespoons parmesan cheese, grated

Preheat oven to 350°.
Have ready a buttered casserole dish.
In a large saucepan, steam zucchini in a basket over simmering water for about 5 minutes, or until crisp-tender. Drain and set aside.
Melt butter in a skillet; add onion and bell pepper; saute until tender. Remove from heat; stir in mushrooms and dry sauce mix.
In a small bowl, mix water and tomato paste until blended; add to skillet and stir. Add zucchini and mozzarella cheese; stir gently. Spoon mixture into the casserole dish and sprinkle with parmesan cheese.
Bake 30-35 minutes.

Baked Beans

2 teaspoons prepared mustard
¼ cup brown sugar
1/3 cup butter or margarine
2 medium onions, chopped
2 cans pork and beans

Preheat oven to 350°.

Combine mustard, sugar, margarine and onions in casserole dish. Add beans and mix. If mixture is too thick, add a couple tablespoons water. Bake for 30-45 minutes, or until onions are tender. Serve warm.

This dish can be used as a side dish or an entrée.

Melba's Best Baked Beans Ever

3 medium cans Bush's® Baked Beans (with brown sugar and onion)
1 bottle Masterpiece® Barbecue Sauce (Honey Smoke)
1 very large yellow onion, chopped
1 tablespoon Lea & Perrins® Worcestershire Sauce
1 tablespoon French's® mustard
1 cup firmly-packed dark brown sugar
1 pound Jimmy Dean® Sage Sausage (must be sage)
Yellow Crisco® for frying

Preheat oven to 350°.

In a cast-iron roaster (preferred) or a heavy Dutch oven, heat Crisco®. Add onion and fry until soft; remove onion from pan and set aside.

Add sausage to pan; fry, breaking meat into small pieces. After sausage is browned, return onion to pan, and add all other ingredients. Mix well.

Bake, uncovered, for 1½ hours.

Note: Melba says, "Beans may seem thin when done but thicken as they cool."

Cheesy Cauliflower

1 large head cauliflower, broken into florets
2 tablespoons butter
2 tablespoons flour
1½ cups evaporated milk
8 ounces Gruyere cheese, shredded
Salt and pepper
4 slices bacon, cooked crisp and crumbled
Parsley leaves

Preheat oven to 300°.

Have ready a buttered casserole dish.

In a large saucepan, steam cauliflower in a basket over simmering water 7-10 minutes, or until barely tender.

In a saucepan over medium heat, melt butter; whisk in flour to make a paste. Stir and cook until paste starts to brown. Whisk in milk and bring mixture to a simmer; cook until thickened, stirring constantly, for 7-10 minutes. Stir in shredded cheese; cook until smooth. Add salt and pepper, to taste.

Remove cauliflower from steamer basket; place in baking dish and pour cheese sauce over florets.

Bake just until cheese sauce starts to brown or use a kitchen torch. Remove from oven.

Garnish with bacon and parsley.

Spinach-Stuffed Tomatoes

1 (10-ounce) package frozen, chopped spinach
¼ cup water
¼ cup mayonnaise
1 tablespoon dried minced onion
1/8 teaspoon ground nutmeg
Salt and pepper, to taste
6 small whole tomatoes
Water, for baking

Preheat oven to 350°.

Have available a small baking dish.

In a small saucepan, bring ¼ cup water to boiling; add spinach. Cook for 3 minutes, stirring to defrost; drain completely.

In same pan, combine spinach with mayonnaise, onion, nutmeg, salt and pepper.

Cut thin slice off top of each tomato and scoop out center; drain upside down on paper towels. Turn tomatoes over and sprinkle inside of each with salt; fill with spinach mixture. Place tomatoes in baking dish; pour hot water ¼ inch deep around tomatoes.

Bake 12-15 minutes.

.

Coconut Rice

½ cup frozen peas, thawed
1 cup long grain white rice
½ teaspoon salt
¼ teaspoon cinnamon
¾ cup coconut milk
1¼ cups water

Preheat oven to 350°.

Butter a 2-quart baking dish; set aside.

In a saucepan, combine the salt, cinnamon, milk, and water; bring to a boil. Pour mixture over peas and rice in baking dish.

Cover and bake for 30 minutes. Check to see if rice is tender. Remove from oven and let stand for 5 minutes. Fluff rice with a fork and serve.

Fried Rice

8 slices bacon, coarsely-chopped
1 (8-ounce) can sliced water chestnuts
4 green onions, sliced thin
1 egg, slightly-beaten
1 cup bean sprouts
1 cup frozen peas, thawed
¼ cup soy sauce
3 cups cooked rice

In a large skillet, cook bacon until crisp. Remove bacon; drain on paper towels on a plate. Pour bacon grease into a heat-safe container. Return 2 tablespoons to skillet; reserve remaining grease to flavor beans or other dishes.

Add water chestnuts and onions to skillet; saute 2 minutes. Add egg; stir until cooked through. Stir in bean sprouts, peas, and soy sauce.

Add cooked rice; stir until everything is heated through.

Red Cucumber Pickles

8 quarts water
2 cups hydrated lime
Cucumbers, peeled
Water
1 cup white or apple cider vinegar
1 tablespoon alum
1 ounce red food coloring

Cut cucumbers in half lengthwise; remove seeds with a spoon or a plastic pill bottle; slice into ¼-inch pieces. In large crock or glass bowl, mix water and lime; add cucumbers and weight down with a heavy plate. Soak 24 hours. Drain and rinse cucumber mixture; soak in ice water; drain again.

*Mix vinegar, alum and food coloring in heavy saucepan; add cucumbers and enough water to cover. Bring mixture to a boil, then simmer 2 hours; remove from heat and drain.

SYRUP STAGE:
2 cups white or apple cider vinegar
2 cups water
10 cups granulated sugar
8 sticks whole cinnamon

Mix vinegar, water and sugar in large saucepan; add cinnamon and drained cucumbers; bring to a boil, then simmer for 45 minutes. Remove from heat and let set overnight. Reheat pickles in syrup; remove from heat and let set overnight. Reheat pickles in syrup; ladle into sterilized jars and seal while hot.

Variation: Use green food coloring instead of red for dark green pickles or divide the mixture into separate saucepans at * and use ½-ounce red food coloring for red pickles and ½-ounce green food coloring for green pickles from the same batch.

Red Pickles a la Shirley & Betty

Cucumbers
Salt
Lime
Water
Vinegar
Sugar
Salt
Red food coloring
Cinnamon
Celery seed, whole cloves, pickling spice

Soak cucumbers 24 hours in mixture, then rinse off.

Mixture:
Handful salt
2 cups lime
1 gallon water.

Soak cucumbers 3 hours in cold, clear water. Rinse.
Cook cucumbers in mixture until clear or transparent, about 40 minutes.

Mixture:
2 quarts vinegar
4¼ pounds sugar
1 tablespoon salt
Red food coloring
2 sticks cinnamon

(Spices in bag):
1 tablespoon celery seed,
1 tablespoon whole cloves,
1 tablespoon pickling spice

Let cool; seal in jars.

14-Day Sweet Pickles

In a clean stone jar, put 2 gallons of cucumbers, washed and sliced. Dissolve 2 cups of salt in 1 gallon of boiling water and pour while hot over cucumbers. Then cover and weight down cucumbers, and let stand one week.

On the eighth day, drain, then pour 1 gallon of boiling water over them, and let stand 24 hours.

On the ninth day, drain, then pour 1 gallon of boiling water with one tablespoon of powdered alum over the cucumbers, and let stand 24 hours.

On the tenth day, drain again. Pour 1 gallon boiling water over the cucumbers, let stand 24 hours, then drain again.

For the pickling mixture, combine 5 pints boiling apple cider vinegar, 6 cups sugar, ½ ounce celery seed, and 1 ounce of cinnamon sticks. Pour this over cucumbers.

Drain off pickling liquid for three mornings, reserving and reheating it, and adding 1 cup sugar each morning.

With the third and last heating, pack pickles into sterilized jars, pour hot liquid over them, and seal.

Note: We never bought pickles. We grew our own pickling cucumbers and made sweet pickles every year – only sweet that we used on hamburgers, in deviled eggs, potato salad, etc. Our 14-day pickles turned into 16 or 17 sometimes. If they weren't sweet or crisp enough, we repeated the reheating and adding 1 cup sugar for extra days. Using large stone crocks, we made large batches. When it came time to heat the pickling liquid, we used a turkey roaster. During the reheating process on the last day of pickling, we added the pickles and heated them in the liquid before we packed them into quart Mason® or Ball® jars.

Deviled Eggs

12 hard-cooked eggs
½ cup mayonnaise
2 tablespoons yellow mustard
1 tablespoon sweet pickle juice
½ cup chopped sweet pickles
½ teaspoon salt
¼ teaspoon black pepper
Paprika

Peel and dry off eggs. Cut each in half, lengthwise. Remove egg yolks to a mixing bowl. Set egg whites aside.

Mash the yolks with mayonnaise, mustard, pickle juice, sweet pickles, salt, and pepper; mix well. With a piping bag, pipe mixture into white halves or spoon mixture into whites with a teaspoon, mounding up mixture in center of each egg half. Sprinkle *lightly* with paprika. Place in a covered container and chill.

Notes: Sweet pickle relish may be substituted for sweet pickles. I prefer Miracle Whip® to plain mayonnaise. Cayenne, hot pepper sauce, Worcestershire sauce, etc. may be added, if desired.

When transporting deviled eggs and you don't have a dedicated egg carrier, halve eggs in the round instead of lengthwise. Fill halves, omit paprika, and press halves together lightly. Place eggs in a plastic egg carton, or paper egg carton lined with plastic wrap, and chill. Later, take with you: carton of deviled eggs, paprika, a disposable plate, knife and fork. At your picnic, or other destination, separate egg halves with knife and place filled halves on plate. Smooth, or round, tops of eggs with knife, and decorate eggs with tines of fork; sprinkle eggs with paprika and serve.

Desserts

Here's what's cookin' P-nut Butter Cookies Serves

Recipe from the kitchen of Irene Pence

1 c. sugar
1 c. peanut butter
1 egg
(2 T honey makes a chewy cookie)

Mix & bake 10-12 min. at 350°

Chocolate Sheath Cake

CAKE BATTER:
- 2 cups granulated sugar
- 2 cups flour
- 1 stick margarine
- ½ cup vegetable shortening
- 4 tablespoons cocoa
- 1 cup hot water
- ½ cup buttermilk
- 1 teaspoon baking soda
- 1 teaspoon vanilla
- Dash salt
- 2 eggs, beaten

Preheat oven to 375°. Grease and flour 13"x9" baking pan or jelly roll pan.

Sift sugar and flour together in large mixing bowl; set aside. Place margarine, shortening, cocoa and water in saucepan; cook until bubbling; pour mixture over dry ingredients and stir. In small mixing bowl, mix buttermilk, soda, vanilla, salt and eggs together; combine this with chocolate mixture; blend well. Pour batter into baking pan and bake 20 minutes, or until done. Remove cake from oven to cool in pan but frost cake while warm.

Warm Chocolate Icing:

- 1 stick margarine
- 4 tablespoons cocoa
- 1 teaspoon vanilla
- 6 tablespoons milk
- 1 pound box powdered sugar
- ¾ cup pecans, chopped

About 5 minutes before cake is done, place margarine, cocoa, vanilla and milk into a small saucepan; bring to a boil. Remove from heat; add powdered sugar, mixing well; stir in nuts. Spread icing on cake while cake is still warm.

Pineapple Upside-Down Cake

1/3 cup butter
½ cup brown sugar
1 (20-ounce) can sliced pineapple, drained
Maraschino cherries, drained
Pecan halves
1 cup sugar
1 1/3 cups flour
2 teaspoons baking powder
½ teaspoon salt
½ cup shortening
2/3 cup milk
1 teaspoon vanilla
1 egg

Preheat oven to 350°.

Melt butter in heavy 10" skillet or baking dish. Sprinkle brown sugar over butter. Place pineapple rings on top of brown sugar. Place cherries in center of pineapple rings and pecan halves, upside down, around pineapple. (Substitution: Drained crushed pineapple instead of sliced; omit cherries and pecans.)

Combine granulated sugar, flour, baking powder and salt in mixing bowl. Add shortening, milk and vanilla; beat 2 minutes with mixer at medium speed or 300 strokes by hand. Add egg and beat 2 more minutes. Pour batter into skillet over pineapple design.

Bake 40-50 minutes. Remove from oven and place a serving plate on top of skillet. Immediately turn skillet upside down on serving plate. Wait a minute or two before lifting skillet straight up from cake. Serve warm.

Queen Elizabeth's Christmas Cake

1 cup boiling water
1 cup dates, chopped
1 teaspoon soda
1 cup butter
1 cup sugar
1 egg, beaten
1½ cups flour
1 teaspoon baking powder
½ teaspoon salt
½ cup candied cherries, chopped
½ cup pecans, chopped

Preheat oven to 350°. Grease an 8x12-inch pan; set aside.
Pour boiling water over dates and soda; let stand until cool. Cream butter and sugar; add beaten egg. Sift together flour, baking powder, and salt. Add dry ingredients to creamed mixture; then add cooked date mixture. Fold in cherries and pecans. Spoon batter into pan and bake for 35 minutes.

ICING:

5 tablespoons brown sugar, packed
5 tablespoons cream or evaporated milk
2 tablespoons butter
½ cup pecans, chopped fine
Whipped cream

Combine brown sugar, cream, and butter in small saucepan. Bring to boil and boil for 3 minutes. Spread icing on cooled cake and sprinkle with pecans. Serve cake with whipped cream.

Note: I am told the queen actually bakes this cake but only once a year. Imagine the royal anticipation!

Sparkling Cider Pound Cake

¾ cup butter, softened
1½ cups granulated sugar
3 eggs
1½ cups flour
¼ teaspoon baking powder
¼ teaspoon salt
½ cup sparkling apple cider
Vegetable shortening (for pan)

Grease a 9x5-inch loaf pan with shortening. Line bottom of pan with parchment paper; grease paper. Set aside.

Preheat oven to 350°.

In a mixing bowl, cream butter and sugar until light and fluffy. Add eggs, one at a time; beat well after each addition.

Whisk flour, baking powder, and salt in a small bowl. Add dry ingredients to creamed mixture, alternating with cider.

Transfer cake batter to loaf pan. Bake 40-50 minutes. Cool in pan for 10 minutes; remove cake to a wire rack to finish cooling.

GLAZE:
1½ cups powdered sugar
6-8 teaspoons sparkling apple cider

In a small bowl, mix powdered sugar and cider until sugar is dissolved. Pour mixture over top of cake, letting it drip over the sides.

Wait for glaze to set up. Slice cake and serve.

Italian Cream Cake

BATTER:
   1 cup buttermilk
   1 teaspoons baking soda
   ½ cup butter
   ½ cup shortening
   2 cups granulated sugar
   5 eggs, separated
   2 cups flour, sifted
   1 teaspoon vanilla
   3½ ounces shredded coconut
   1 cup pecans, chopped

Preheat oven to 350°.
Grease and flour 3 (9-inch) cake pans; set aside.
Mix soda in buttermilk; set aside. In the large mixing bowl of an electric mixer, cream butter, shortening, and sugar. Add egg yolks, one at time, beating well after each one. Add buttermilk and flour alternately, mixing well. Stir in vanilla. Set mixture aside.

In a different bowl, beat egg whites to stiff peaks; fold into cake batter. Stir in coconut and pecans.

Bake 25 minutes. Cool layers on wire racks.

FROSTING:
   1 (8-ounce) package cream cheese, softened
   1 cup butter, softened
   8 cups powdered sugar
   3 teaspoons vanilla
   1½ cups pecans, chopped

With an electric mixer, cream butter and cream cheese in large mixing bowl. Beat in all of the powdered sugar, a little at a time, until it reaches spreading consistency. Stir in vanilla and pecans. Frost cake layers.

Quick German Chocolate Cake

1 cup shredded coconut
1 cup nuts, coarsely-chopped
1 box German Chocolate Cake Mix
Water and/or eggs – as called for on cake mix box
½ cup butter or margarine
8 ounces cream cheese
1 box powdered sugar

Preheat oven to 350°.

Spray 9x13-inch cake pan with cooking spray. Spread coconut and pecans evenly in bottom of pan; set aside.

Prepare cake-mix batter according to directions on box. Pour batter over nut mixture in cake pan.

In a small saucepan over low heat, melt butter and cream cheese. Remove from heat and add sugar. Beat by hand until smooth. Pour, or dollop, mixture over cake. (This mixture will not incorporate completely. Do not spread to edge of pan. Let it go where it wants.)

Bake 35-40 minutes. Let cool in pan.

Carrot Cake

BATTER:
- 2 cups flour
- 1 teaspoon baking soda
- 1 teaspoon baking powder
- ¼ teaspoon salt
- 1 teaspoon cinnamon
- 2 cups sugar
- 1½ cups salad oil
- 4 eggs
- 2 cups carrots, finely grated

Preheat oven to 350°.

Grease and flour three 8-inch cake pans. Set aside.

Sift together flour, baking soda, baking powder, salt, and cinnamon; set aside.

In a large mixing bowl, mix sugar and oil. Add eggs, one at a time, beating well after each addition. Add dry ingredients gradually, mixing well. Add carrots; stir until incorporated. Pour mixture evenly into prepared pans.

Bake 50-60 minutes. Remove cakes from oven and let cool before frosting with Nut Icing.

NUT ICING:
- ½ cup butter or margarine
- 1 (8-ounce) package cream cheese
- 1 box (1-pound) powdered sugar
- 1 teaspoon vanilla
- 1 cup nuts, chopped

In a small mixing bowl, beat butter and cream cheese until light in color. Continue beating, adding sugar gradually. Add vanilla and nuts; beat to blend. Frost cake layers and serve.

Banana Cake

2 cups flour
¼ teaspoon baking powder
¾ teaspoon baking soda
½ teaspoon salt
½ cup shortening
1½ cups sugar
2 eggs
1 cup mashed bananas
¼ cup sour milk
1 teaspoon vanilla
1 cup nuts, chopped

Preheat oven to 350°. Grease and flour a 9-inch loaf pan; set aside.

Sift flour, baking powder, baking soda, and salt. Set aside.

In a mixing bowl, cream shortening and sugar. Beat in eggs. Add dry ingredients; mix well. Add bananas, milk, vanilla, and nuts. Beat until well blended. Pour batter into prepared pan.

Bake 30-35 minutes. Let cool in pan.

Banana Split Cake

2 cups graham cracker crumbs
3 sticks margarine, softened (divided)
2 cups powdered sugar
2 eggs
1 cup crushed pineapple, drained
4 bananas, sliced in rounds
1 (8-ounce) carton whipped topping
½ cup Maraschino cherries, chopped fine
½ cup pecans, chopped fine

In a small bowl, mix crumbs with 1 stick of margarine. Spread mixture in bottom of 9x13-inch pan. (I like a glass or ceramic pan.)

In a mixing bowl, combine 2 sticks margarine, sugar, and eggs; mix for 15 minutes. Spread filling over crumb mixture.

Spread a layer of pineapple over filling and top with banana slices.

Cover cake with whipped topping and sprinkle with cherries and nuts to garnish. Cover pan with plastic wrap and place in refrigerator.

For serving, cut cake into squares and serve chilled.

Red Velvet Cake

1½ cups sugar
½ cup shortening
2 eggs
1 teaspoon vanilla
1 teaspoon butter flavor
1 ounce liquid red food color
3 tablespoons cocoa
2½ cups cake flour
1 teaspoon salt
1 teaspoon baking soda
1 cup buttermilk
1 tablespoon vinegar

Preheat oven to 350°.

Have ready 3 greased and floured 8-inch (or 9-inch) cake pans.

In a mixing bowl of an electric mixer, cream sugar and shortening until light and fluffy. Add eggs, one at a time, beating vigorously after each addition. Add flavorings.

Make a paste of food color and cocoa; blend into cake mixture.

Sift together flour, salt, and soda; add alternately with buttermilk, mixing well. Add vinegar; beat only until smooth.

Bake 20-25 minutes. Remove cake layers from oven and cool on wire racks for 10 minutes. Remove cake layers from pans; cool completely.

Frost between layers and frost top of cake with your favorite frosting and serve.

Parfait Cake

1 box white cake mix
Water and/or eggs – as called for on cake mix box
1 small package strawberry Jello®
Water
1 container whipped topping
1 pound fresh strawberries, sliced

Preheat oven to temperature stated on cake mix box.

Spray 9x13-inch cake pan with baking spray; set aside.

Prepare cake-mix batter according to directions on box. Pour batter into prepared pan; bake according to directions on box.

Prepare Jello® powder as directed on its box; set aside.

When cake has baked, remove from oven; let cool Punch lots of holes in cake with a fork with large tines. Pour Jello® liquid over cake. Chill in refrigerator.

When cake is chilled, mix whipped topping with strawberries and spread on cake. Return to refrigerator; keep cake chilled.

Zucchini Chocolate Cake

2½ cups flour
1 teaspoon baking soda
1 teaspoon salt
¼ cup cocoa
½ cup butter
½ cup cooking oil
1¾ cups sugar
2 eggs
1 teaspoon vanilla
½ cup milk
2 cups zucchini, grated with peeling on
1 (6-ounce) package chocolate chips
¾ cup walnuts, chopped

Preheat oven to 325°. Grease a 9x13-inch baking pan; set aside.
Sift flour, soda, salt, and cocoa together; set aside.

In a large mixing bowl, cream butter, oil, and sugar until light and fluffy. Add eggs and vanilla; beat well. Add dry ingredients and milk, beat well. Stir in zucchini. Pour batter into prepared pan. Sprinkle with chocolate chips and nuts.

Bake 55 minutes. Cool in pan on a wire rack.

Cut cake into squares. Will serve 16.

Almond Streusel Coffee Cake

STREUSEL:
- 1 cup light brown sugar, packed
- 1 cup sliced almonds
- ¼ cup flour
- 3 tablespoons butter, melted
- 1 teaspoon grated orange zest

In a medium bowl, combine brown sugar, almonds, and flour. Stir in butter and orange zest; set aside.

Preheat oven to 350°. Have ready a greased tube pan.

CAKE BATTER:
- 2 cups flour
- 1 teaspoon baking powder
- 1 teaspoon baking soda
- 1 stick butter
- ½ cup granulated sugar
- 3 large eggs
- 1 teaspoon grated orange zest
- ½ teaspoon vanilla
- 2/3 cup orange juice

Combine flour, baking powder and baking soda; set aside.

In a large bowl of an electric mixer, beat butter and sugar on medium speed until fluffy. Add eggs, one at a time, beating well after each addition. Stir in orange zest and vanilla. On low speed, add dry ingredients alternately with 2/3 cup orange juice, beating after each addition. (Always start and end with dry.)

Spoon half of batter into prepared pan. Sprinkle with half of streusel mixture. Cover with remaining batter and streusel.

Bake 30-35 minutes, or until a toothpick inserted in center of cake comes out clean. Transfer pan to wire rack to cool completely. Remove cake from pan; turn cake right-side up on a serving plate.

GLAZE:

In a small bowl, mix ½ cup powdered sugar and 2½ teaspoons orange juice. Drizzle cake with glaze.

Orange-Glazed Coffee Cake

1 package dry yeast
¼ cup water, warmed to 110°
½ cup milk, warmed to 110°
½ cup orange juice
½ cup sugar
½ teaspoon salt
½ cup ricotta cheese
1 tablespoon grated orange zest
1 egg, slightly beaten + 1 egg to brush on dough
3½ -4 cups flour
1 cup powdered sugar + 2 tablespoons orange juice, for Glaze

Grease a 10-inch springform pan and a large bowl; set aside.

In a different bowl, the large bowl of an electric mixer, dissolve yeast in warm water. Let stand until foamy, 5-10 minutes. Stir in warm milk, orange juice, sugar, salt, cheese, orange zest, and 1 egg.

Using paddle attachment and mixer at low speed, beat 2 cups flour into the yeast and egg mixture until a wet dough forms. Beat in the remaining flour, ½ cup at a time, until a stiff dough forms.

Turn dough out onto a lightly-floured surface and knead 5-10 minutes, until dough is smooth and elastic. If dough sticks, add more flour, a tiny amount at a time.

Place dough in greased bowl, turning to coat top of dough. Cover bowl loosely with a damp cloth; let rise in a warm place until doubled, about 1½ hours.

Punch down the dough with your closed fist. Turn dough out onto a lightly-floured surface and knead for 1-2 minutes. Divide dough into 3 equal portions. Roll each piece into a 20-inch-long rope. Braid ropes together.

Coil braided dough in prepared pan, tucking ends under. Cover loosely with damp cloth; let rise 30 minutes, or until almost doubled.

Preheat oven to 425°.

Beat second egg with a fork; brush dough with egg. Bake 25-30 minutes until cake is golden. Remove to a wire rack to cool slightly.

In a small bowl, mix powdered sugar and orange juice. Spread over warm cake. Serve immediately.

Yum Yum Cake

1 cake mix + required ingredients (eggs, oil, and/or water)
1 box vanilla pudding mix
1 cup milk
1 (8-ounce) package cream cheese, softened
1 (8-ounce) container whipped topping, thawed
1 (20-ounce) can crushed pineapple, drained
Shredded coconut
Chopped nuts

Choose a yellow, pineapple, or lemon cake mix.

Preheat oven to temperature suggested on cake mix box. Grease and flour a jelly roll pan.

Pour dry cake mix into a large mixing bowl; add ingredients, such as eggs, oil, water, etc. following directions on cake mix box. Beat well and pour batter into jelly roll pan. Bake for approximately 20 minutes, or until done. Remove cake from oven and let cool in pan; set aside.

Cook pudding mix in small saucepan with only 1 cup milk, following other directions on pudding box. Remove from heat and let cool; set aside.

In a small bowl, combine cream cheese and whipped topping; blend well. Stir in pudding and mix well; spread on cooled cake. Top this mixture with pineapple, then sprinkle with coconut and nuts. Refrigerate before serving.

Dump Cake

1 large can crushed pineapple
1 large can cherry pie filling
1 box yellow or white cake mix
½ cup nuts, chopped
1-2 sticks butter or margarine
Whipped cream topping

Preheat oven to 350°. Grease a 13"x9" baking pan.

Pour pineapple and juice into pan. Pour cherry pie filling on top of pineapple. On top of cherries, sprinkle dry cake mix; sprinkle nuts over cake mix. Slice butter into very thin slices and lay on top of nuts and dry cake mix. *One stick is recommended, but I found it too dry and used both sticks of butter.* Bake cake for one hour. Cool and serve with whipped topping.

Dream Cake

1 cake mix
½ cup salad oil
1 vanilla instant pudding mix
4 eggs
1 cup water
1 cup powdered sugar
2 tablespoons milk

Preheat oven to 350°. Grease and flour a tube pan.

Combine all ingredients in a large bowl; mix well. Pour batter into tube pan. Bake for 45-55 minutes, or until done. Remove from oven and let cake cool slightly; remove cake from pan and place on a round cake plate or large dinner plate.

In small bowl, mix powdered sugar with milk; spread glaze over warm cake.

Oatmeal Cake

1¼ cup boiling water
1 cup quick-cooking oats
1 cup light brown sugar
1 cup granulated sugar
½ cup vegetable shortening or butter
2 eggs, slightly beaten
11/3 cup flour
½ teaspoon salt
1 teaspoon baking soda
1 teaspoon ground cinnamon
1 teaspoon vanilla

Preheat oven to 350°. Grease bottom of 15'x10'x2' cake pan.

Pour boiling water over oats in small bowl; let stand while mixing other ingredients. Cream sugars with shortening in large mixing bowl; add eggs and beat until well blended. Sift flour, salt, soda and cinnamon; add to creamed mixture and beat. Stir in oats and vanilla. Pour into pan; bake 30-40 minutes. Frost with icing while hot.

Icing for Oatmeal Cake

1 cup light brown sugar
¾ stick margarine
1 cup shredded coconut
1 cup pecans, chopped (optional)
1 teaspoon vanilla

Cream brown sugar and margarine; add coconut, nuts and vanilla. Do not cook. Pour over hot cake and spread evenly. Put pan under broiler for 2 minutes. Remove from oven; let cool before serving.

Lemon Jello® Cake

1 package yellow cake mix
1 package lemon Jello® gelatin
¾ cup salad oil
4 eggs
1 tablespoon lemon extract
¾ cup water
1 cup powdered sugar
3 tablespoons lemon juice

Preheat oven to 350°. Grease and flour a 13"x9" baking pan.

Combine cake mix and gelatin in mixer bowl; add salad oil and 2 eggs; mix well. Add remaining 2 eggs, lemon extract and water; beat until well-blended. Pour batter into baking pan; bake for 30 minutes or until done. Remove cake from oven and glaze while still warm.

For glaze: Mix powdered sugar and lemon juice together; pour over cake. Let cool and serve.

Mississippi Mud Cake

CAKE BATTER:
   2 sticks margarine or butter
   2 cups sugar
   3 tablespoons cocoa
   4 eggs
   1 teaspoon vanilla
   1½ cups flour
   2 cups shredded coconut
   1 cup pecans, chopped

Preheat oven to 350°. Grease and flour a 13"x9" baking pan.

Cream margarine, sugar and cocoa in mixer bowl; beat in eggs and vanilla. Add flour, coconut and nuts; mix well. Pour batter into baking pan; bake 30-40 minutes or until done. Remove cake from oven; leave cake in pan.

TOPPING:
   1 jar marshmallow crème

Immediately spread marshmallow crème over hot cake. Let cake cool completely before frosting.

FROSTING:
   1 pound box powdered sugar
   1 stick margarine or butter
   ½ cup evaporated milk
   1/3 cup cocoa
   1 teaspoon vanilla

Beat powdered sugar, margarine, milk, cocoa and vanilla together; pour over marshmallow crème on top of cake. Let cool and serve.

Easy Peach Cobbler

1/3 cup sugar
1 large can sliced peaches (#2½)
1 cup flour
1 cup sugar
1½ teaspoons baking powder
¼ teaspoon salt
½ cup milk
1 stick (½ cup) margarine

Preheat oven to 350°.

Heat 1/3 cup sugar and peaches in saucepan until sugar is dissolved; set aside.

Combine flour, 1 cup sugar, baking powder, salt, and milk in a small bowl; mix well with spoon and set aside.

Put margarine in a 12"x7"x1½" baking dish; put in oven until butter melts. Remove and swirl margarine to coat bottom of dish. Pour batter over margarine; *do not stir.*

Place sliced peaches on top of batter and pour all of the juice evenly over batter; *do not stir.*

Bake for 45 minutes or until golden brown.

Serve warm.

*Note: **Easy** recipe above is one I make often.*

***Quick** recipe below came from Grandma Dory. It uses a dry cake mix instead of a mixed batter. Randy and Cathy make it.*

Quick Peach Cobbler

1 large can peaches
1 cake mix (white or yellow)
1 cube of butter

Put peaches in cake pan. Empty cake mix over peaches. Cut the butter in pieces over mix.

Bake.

Peach juice will bubble up through mix.

Cherry Crunch

CRUST:
    1½ sticks butter or margarine
    40 graham crackers, crushed (about 3 cups)
    ¾ cup sugar
    1 teaspoon cinnamon

Preheat oven to only 275°. Butter bottom of 13"x9" glass baking pan.

Melt butter; mix with cracker crumbs, sugar and cinnamon. Pat ¾ of mixture in bottom of pan.

FILLING:
    1 quart cherries (2 cans)
    1½ cups sugar
    5 tablespoons cornstarch

Mix cornstarch and sugar with cherries (including juice) in saucepan; cook until mixture is thick and clear. While hot, pour over crumb crust.

TOPPING:
    5 egg whites
    1 cup sugar

Beat egg whites in large mixing bowl with sugar until stiff; spread this mixture over cherries. Top with remaining crumb/crust mixture. Bake 30-35 minutes. Remove from oven and let cool; serve. Refrigerate leftovers; serve chilled.

Soda Cracker Torte

3 egg whites
1 teaspoon vanilla
½ teaspoon salt
1 cup granulated sugar
¾ cup chopped walnuts
¾ cup coarsely-crushed soda crackers
1 teaspoon baking powder
1 cup heavy whipping cream
Sugar, for topping

Preheat oven to 350°.
Have ready a greased 8-inch square pan.
In the mixing bowl of an electric mixer, beat egg whites with vanilla and salt until frothy. Slowly add sugar, beating until stiff; set aside.
In a small bowl, combine walnuts, crushed crackers, and baking powder. Add to meringue mixture; fold in and set aside.
Fill a clean sink or a container large enough to hold the 8-inch pan with cold water. Dip pan in cold water; lift and shake off water droplets.
Spoon cracker/meringue into pan.
Bake 35-40 minutes. Remove from oven and let cool.
In a small bowl, whip cream while adding sugar to sweeten to your taste. Spread over baked torte. Place in refrigerator to chill at least 8 hours before serving.

Pumpkin-Pecan Pie

1 egg, slightly beaten
1 cup pumpkin
1/3 cup sugar
½ teaspoon cinnamon
¼ teaspoon ginger
1/8 teaspoon cloves
1 (9-inch) prepared pie shell

In a small mixing bowl, combine first 6 ingredients; pour mixture into pie shell. Set aside.
Preheat oven to 350°.

2 eggs, slightly beaten
2/3 cup corn syrup (light or dark)
2/3 cup sugar
2 tablespoons margarine, melted
½ teaspoon vanilla
1 cup pecans

In a mixing bowl, combine eggs, syrup, sugar, margarine, and vanilla; mix well. Stir in pecans. Pour mixture into pastry-lined pie pan. Bake for 1 hour. Let cool before serving.

Pecan Pie

3 eggs
2/3 cup sugar
½ teaspoon salt
1 cup light corn syrup
1/3 cup butter, melted
1 cup pecan halves
Pastry for 9" pie

Preheat oven to 375°. Combine eggs, sugar, salt, syrup and butter in mixing bowl; beat with a whisk or a rotary beater. Stir in pecans. Pour mixture into pastry-lined pie pan. Bake 40-50 minutes or until set and crust is browned. Let cool.

Pina Colada Surprise Pie

1 can sweetened condensed milk
1 (10-ounce) can pina colada mix
1 (20-ounce) can crushed pineapple
1 cup chopped pecans
1 (14-ounce) package angel flake coconut (reserve ½ cup)
1 (12-ounce) + 1 (8-ounce) container whipped topping
1 (9-inch) prepared graham cracker crust

In a mixing bowl, combine condensed milk, pina colada mix, pineapple, pecans, coconut except for reserve, and 12 ounces of whipped topping; mix well. Pour mixture into prepared pie shell.

Spread 8 ounces of whipped topping on top of pie. Sprinkle reserved coconut on top.

Chill at least 3 hours before serving.

Lemonade Pie

1 can sweetened condensed milk
1 small can frozen lemonade or pink lemonade
1 (8-ounce) container whipped topping
1 (9-inch) prepared pastry shell or graham cracker crust

In a mixing bowl, combine condensed milk, (thawed) lemonade concentrate, and whipped topping. Pour mixture into prepared crust. Chill at least 3 hours before serving.

Vanilla Ice Cream

2¼ cups sugar
6 tablespoons flour
½ teaspoon salt
5 cups whole milk, scalded
6 eggs, lightly beaten
4 cups heavy cream
4½ teaspoons vanilla

Combine sugar, flour, and salt in a saucepan. Slowly stir in hot milk; cook over low heat, stirring constantly, for 10 minutes or until thickened. Mix small amount of hot mixture into bowl of beaten eggs to temper them. Add back to saucepan and cook 1 minute. Place in refrigerator to chill.

When chilled, add heavy cream and vanilla; pour into can of ice cream freezer. Following freezer directions, process mixture until frozen.

Serve immediately

Variations:
1. **Chocolate Chip Ice Cream** – After churning for 15 minutes, add 1 and 2/3 cups grated or chopped semi-sweet chocolate. Resume freezing.
2. **Peppermint Candy Ice Cream** – After churning for 15 minutes, add 1½ cups crushed peppermint candies. Resume freezing.
3. **Egg Nog Ice Cream** – Add 1 teaspoon ground nutmeg and add 2 tablespoons rum flavoring instead of vanilla.
4. **Butter Nut Ice Cream** – After churning for 15 minutes, add 2 cups pecans, walnuts, or almonds that have been sauted in 3 tablespoons butter and cooled. Resume freezing.

Berry-Berry Cool Pops

½ cup fresh strawberries, sliced
½ cup fresh berries (blackberries, raspberries or blueberries)
2 cups juice (white grape, pineapple or apple)
1 (8-ounce) can crushed pineapple

Divide mixed berries and drop into 12 freezer pop molds; set aside.

In a blender, combine juice and undrained pineapple. Cover and blend until smooth. Pour over fruit in freezer molds. Insert plastic sticks through slits in top of each mold; cover and place in freezer.

Freeze at least 6 hours.

To serve, remove frozen pops from freezer, and unmold. Serve immediately.

Variation:

Berries and juices may be combined for creative flavor treats.

Twelve small paper cups may be substituted for freezer pop molds. Divide berries and pour blended mixture into paper cups. Cover each cup with aluminum foil. With the tip of a sharp knife, cut a slit in the center of each foil top and insert a wooden craft stick, or a plastic spoon, in each cup. Place cups in freezer.

Freeze at least 6 hours.

To serve, remove frozen pops from freezer; remove foil and tear away paper cups. Serve immediately.

Applesauce Cookies

1 egg
¾ cup shortening
1 cup brown sugar, packed
¾ cup applesauce
2 ¼ cups flour
½ teaspoon baking soda
½ teaspoon salt
1 teaspoon cinnamon
¼ teaspoon ground cloves (optional)
1 cup raisins or dried cranberries
1 cup walnuts, chopped

Preheat oven to 375°. Whisk together egg, shortening and sugar in a mixing bowl; stir in applesauce. Add flour, baking soda, salt, cinnamon, and cloves, if desired; mixing just until blended with a wooden spoon. Stir in raisins, or cranberries, and walnuts. Drop batter by tablespoon onto an ungreased baking sheet; bake 10-12 minutes. (Do not overbake; cookies will be soft on top.) Remove baking sheet from oven and place cookies on a cooling rack.

Magic Cookie Bars

½ cup butter or margarine
1½ cups graham cracker crumbs
1 (14-ounce) can Eagle® Brand Sweetened Condensed Milk
1 (6-ounce) package semi-sweet chocolate chips
1 1/3 cups flaked coconut (or a 3½-ounce can)
1 cup nuts, chopped

Preheat oven to 350°.

Melt butter in 9x13-inch baking pan in oven. Sprinkle crumbs over butter; pour condensed milk evenly over crumbs. Top with chocolate chips, coconut, and nuts; press down firmly.

Bake for 25-30 minutes. Remove from oven and let cool.

Cut cookies into bars and serve. To store cookie bars, cover loosely and store at room temperature.

Five-Layer Bars

1 (10-ounce) package soft coconut macaroon cookies
½ cup sweetened condensed milk
6 tablespoons semi-sweet chocolate chips or chunks
6 tablespoons dried cranberries or raisins
½ cup peanuts, coarsely chopped
Vegetable shortening

Preheat oven to 350°.

Grease a 2-quart baking dish with vegetable shortening.

Unwrap cookies and place into prepared baking dish. Press cookies together to make a crust in the bottom of the dish.

Bake for 12 minutes. Remove from oven.

Drizzle crust with condensed milk. Sprinkle with chocolate pieces, cranberries or raisins, and peanuts.

Bake for 25 minutes or until edges start to brown. Remove from oven, let cool in pan on a wire rack. When cookies are cool, cut into 15 bars and serve.

Basic Brownies

4 eggs
2 cups sugar
2/3 cup cocoa
1 cup vegetable shortening
1½ cups flour
2 teaspoons vanilla
Pinch of salt
1½ cups pecans or walnuts, chopped

Preheat oven to 350°. Butter 13"x9" pan.

Place all ingredients in large bowl; mix well with a spoon. Pour mixture into pan and bake about 30 minutes, or until no longer gooey in the center. Let cool until set; serve warm or cold, plain or frosted with a chocolate icing.

Variation: Makes a good base for a serving of vanilla ice cream, topped with a hot fudge sauce.

Eggnog Cheesecake Bars

CRUST:
  1 cup graham cracker crumbs
  3 tablespoons sugar
  ¼ teaspoon ginger
  ¼ teaspoon cinnamon
  ¼ teaspoon nutmeg
  3 tablespoons butter, melted

Preheat oven to 375°.

Line an 8x8x2-inch baking pan with foil or parchment paper; set aside.

In a medium bowl, combine crumbs, sugar, ginger, cinnamon, and nutmeg. Add butter; mix with a fork. Pour crumb mixture into prepared pan; press into an even crust.

Bake 5 minutes. Remove pan from oven and let crust cool.

Reduce oven temperature to 325°.

FILLING:
  12 ounces cream cheese, softened
  1/3 cup sugar
  1 egg
  ¾ cup eggnog
  2 tablespoons graham cracker crumbs

In a large mixing bowl of an electric mixer, beat cream cheese on medium-high speed 1 minute, or until smooth. Add sugar; beat another minute. Beat in egg until mixture is smooth. Add eggnog and beat one minute more on medium speed.

Pour filling over cooled crust. Bake 25-30 minutes at 325° or until center is set. Remove from oven; cool 1 hour in pan on wire rack. Cover and chill in refrigerator at least 4 hours.

When ready to serve, cut into 16 bars. Garnish center of each bar with crumbs.

Eggnog-Macadamia Bars

2 cups sugar
2/3 cup butter
1 teaspoon vanilla
2 eggs
2 cups flour
1 teaspoon baking powder
½ teaspoon nutmeg
1 cup chopped macadamia nuts
1 tablespoon eggnog
1 cup powdered sugar
Vegetable shortening

Preheat oven to 350°. Line a 9x13-inch baking pan with foil; grease foil; set aside.

In a medium saucepan, stir sugar and butter together. Cook over medium heat, stirring until butter melts and sugar is dissolved. Remove from heat and cool slightly.

Stir vanilla and eggs into sugar mixture. Stir in flour, baking powder, and nutmeg. Stir in nuts.

Spoon mixture into prepared pan, spreading evenly. Bake 25-30 minutes when edges begin to pull away from sides of pan. Cool in pan on a wire rack.

Grasp foil to remove bars from pan; place on counter or cutting board; cut into 36 diamond bars. Drizzle with eggnog glaze.

Eggnog Glaze

2 tablespoons eggnog
1 cup powdered sugar
¼ teaspoon vanilla

In a small bowl, combine 1 tablespoon eggnog, powdered sugar, and vanilla; mix well. Add more eggnog at a time, 1 teaspoon at a time, beating after each addition until glaze mixture reaches drizzling consistency. Drizzle glaze over bars with a fork.

Marshmallow Treats

¼ cup butter or margarine
4 cups miniature marshmallows
5 cups Kellogg's® Rice Krispies cereal
Butter

Butter a 9x13x2-inch baking pan. Set aside.

Melt ¼ cup butter or margarine in a large saucepan over low heat. Add marshmallows and stir until completely melted. Cook over low heat 3 minutes longer, stirring constantly. Remove pan from heat.

Add cereal; stir until well coated. Press mixture into prepared baking pan. (Use a buttered spatula or a piece of waxed paper to make pressing easier.) Let mixture cool.

Cut into squares. (Will yield 24 2x2-inch squares.)

Variations:

Marshmallow Snowmen and **Marshmallow Snowballs**

For snowmen, shape cereal mixture while warm into round balls, using toothpicks to hold the pieces together. Decorate with candies, coconut, frosting, and marshmallows to create facial features and buttons. Use licorice strips for a broom.

For snowballs, shape cereal mixture while warm into balls and roll them in coconut.

Payday Cookies

1 cup sugar
1 cup white corn syrup
1 cup peanut butter
1 cup roasted peanuts
1 teaspoon vanilla
1 (10-13-ounce) box corn flakes

Have ready a small bowl of water and a cookie sheet.

Stir sugar and syrup together in a saucepan; bring a boil. Remove from heat and add peanut butter, stirring until smooth.

Add peanuts, vanilla, and most of the corn flakes. (It may not take the entire box of corn flakes.)

Stir until the corn flakes are well coated.

Place mixture onto a cookie sheet and press flat. (Dip hands in cold water for pressing). Let mixture cool completely.

To serve, cut into squares. Keep in a covered container.

Pumpkin Cookies

½ cup shortening
1 cup sugar
1 cup canned pumpkin
1 egg
1 cup raisins or chopped dates
½ cup nuts, chopped
2 cups flour, sifted
1 teaspoon baking powder
½ teaspoon salt
1 teaspoon baking soda
1 teaspoon cinnamon

Preheat oven to 375°.

In a mixing bowl, stir together shortening, sugar, pumpkin, and egg. Add raisins or dates and nuts. Blend in dry ingredients.

Drop batter by teaspoonfuls on cookie sheet. Bake 10-15 minutes.

Remove from oven and let cookies cool on a wire rack.

Lemon Cookies

2 tablespoons shortening
¼ cup milk
1 egg
1 teaspoon lemon juice
1 teaspoon lemon peel, grated
1 cup flour
½ cup sugar
½ teaspoon salt
2 teaspoons baking powder

Preheat oven to 375°. Grease a cookie sheet and set aside.

In a mixing bowl, stir together shortening, milk, egg, lemon juice and peel. Add flour, sugar, salt, and baking powder. Beat until smooth.

Drop batter about 3 inches apart by teaspoonfuls on the cookie sheet.

Bake for 10-12 minutes.

Remove from oven and let cookies cool on a wire rack.

Note: Recipe makes 30 low-calorie cookies – 40 calories per cookie.

Hawaiian Drop Cookies

2 cups flour
2 teaspoons baking powder
½ teaspoon salt
2/3 cup shortening
1¼ cups granulated sugar
1 egg
¾ cup crushed pineapple
½ teaspoon vanilla
½ teaspoon almond extract
½ cup shredded coconut

Preheat oven to 325°.

In a small bowl, combine flour, baking powder, and salt; set aside.

In a mixing bowl, cream shortening and sugar. Add egg and beat well. Blend in pineapple, vanilla, and almond extract. Mix in dry ingredients.

Drop batter by teaspoonfuls on cookie sheet and sprinkle with coconut.

Bake 20 minutes.

Remove from oven and let cookies cool on a wire rack.

Cowboy Cookies

2 cups flour
1 teaspoon baking soda
½ teaspoon baking powder
½ teaspoon salt
1 cup shortening
1 cup granulated sugar
1 cup firmly-packed brown sugar
2 eggs
1 teaspoon vanilla
2 cups rolled oats
12 ounces semi-sweet chocolate chips

Preheat oven to 350°.

Have ready baking sheets sprayed with cooking spray.

In a medium bowl, sift together flour, baking soda, baking powder, and salt; set aside.

In a large bowl, cream shortening, sugars, eggs, and vanilla until light and fluffy. Add flour mixture; mix well. Stir in oats and chocolate chips. Drop mixture with teaspoons onto prepared backing sheets.

Bake 12 to 15 minutes, or until lightly browned. Remove cookies to wire racks to cool completely.

Chocolate Chunk Cookies

1 cup flaked coconut
1 cup pecans
2 (4-ounce) packages German's® Sweet Chocolate®
1 cup flour
½ teaspoon baking powder
¼ teaspoon salt
½ cup butter
½ cup brown sugar, packed
1 egg
1 teaspoon vanilla

Preheat oven to 350°.

Toast coconut and pecans in shallow pan for 7-8 minutes; set aside to cool. Chop pecans.

Raise oven temperature to 375°.

Chop half of chocolate; set aside. Melt remaining chocolate in a double boiler; set aside.

Combine flour, baking powder, and salt; set aside.

Beat butter and sugar in large bowl with mixer until light and fluffy. Add egg and vanilla; mix well. Blend in melted chocolate. Gradually add flour mixture, mixing well after each addition. Stir in coconut, nuts, and chopped chocolate.

Drop heaping tablespoons of dough, 2 inches apart, onto baking sheets.

Bake 10 minutes, or until cookies are puffed and feel set to the touch. Cool on baking sheets for 1 minute. Remove cookies to wire racks; cool completely.

Chocolate Brownie Drops

2 (4-ounce) packages German's® Sweet Chocolate®
1 tablespoon butter
¼ cup flour
¼ teaspoon baking powder
1/8 teaspoon salt
2 eggs
¾ cup sugar
¾ cup pecans, finely-chopped
½ teaspoon vanilla

Preheat oven to 350°.

Melt chocolate and butter in a double boiler; stir and set aside to cool.

Combine flour, baking powder, and salt; set aside.

In a mixing bowl, beat eggs with an electric mixer until foamy. Add sugar, 2 tablespoons at a time; beat until thickened – about 5 minutes. Stir in chocolate and dry ingredients; blend well. Stir in nuts and vanilla. Drop cookie dough by teaspoon onto greased baking sheet.

Bake in oven 8-10 minutes, until cookies feel set when touched lightly. Do not overbake; cookies will be hard as a rock.

Apple-Date Cookies

½ cup margarine
1 cup sugar
1 egg, slightly beaten
1 cup applesauce
2 cups flour
1 teaspoon baking soda
1 teaspoon salt
1 teaspoon cinnamon
1 cup dates, chopped
1 cup nuts, chopped

Preheat oven to 350°.

Cream margarine and sugar well in mixing bowl. Add egg and applesauce; blend. Add flour, soda, salt and cinnamon; mix well. Stir in dates and nuts. Drop by spoonfuls onto ungreased baking sheet and bake for 12 minutes. Remove from oven and place cookies on a wire rack to cool.

When you have unexpected company or a pot-luck dish you forgot to prepare, this is the quickest and easiest recipe to make: no shortening to measure or cream; no need to pack brown sugar into a measuring cup; most items are in your pantry; can mix with a spoon; only four ingredients in the cookie dough; fast to throw together but tastes like you worked really hard in the kitchen.

Jewish Cookies

COOKIE BATTER:
> 4 large eggs
> 1 16-ounce package light brown sugar
> 1½ cups flour
> ½ cup nuts, chopped coarsely
> Butter (for pan)

Preheat oven to 350°. Butter a 13"x9" cake pan and set aside. Mix eggs, sugar, flour, and nuts; pour (thick) batter into pan.
> Bake 30 minutes. Remove pan from oven.

TOPPING:
> ¼ cup evaporated milk
> ½ cup powdered sugar
> 1 teaspoon cinnamon

During the last 5 minutes of baking time, mix milk, sugar and cinnamon together in a small bowl; set aside. When cookies are out of the oven, pour topping over hot cookies in pan. Let cookies cool in pan. Cut into squares and serve.

Note: I've made this cookie since my teens but never knew the origin of the name. Over the years, I've donated the recipe to dozens of cookbooks. Some of the editors changed the name to Chewy Cookies, so you may already make these cookies.

Our favorite chocolate chip cookie recipe – I always triple it. Extra cookie dough may be wrapped tightly and placed in the freezer to be baked later or added to vanilla ice cream, if you're a fan of cookie-dough ice cream. Baked cookies may also be frozen.

Chocolate Chip Cookies

1 cup shortening
½ cup granulated sugar
1 cup tightly-packed light brown sugar
1 teaspoon vanilla
2 large eggs, beaten with a fork
2 cups + 4 tablespoons flour
1 teaspoon baking soda
1 teaspoon salt
2 cups chocolate chips
2 cups pecans or walnuts, chopped

Preheat oven to 375°. (No need to grease cookie sheets.)

In small bowl, combine flour, soda and salt; set aside. Cream shortening, sugars and vanilla in large bowl with electric mixer. Beat in eggs. Add dry ingredients; mix until blended. Stir in chips and nuts. Using two teaspoons, drop batter onto cookie sheet; bake for 10 minutes. Remove from oven; let set 1 minute. With spatula, remove cookies to wire racks to cool. Serve warm or at room temperature.

Our favorite peanut butter cookie recipe – I always triple this. Baked cookies may be wrapped tightly and frozen. Keep a few in a sandwich-sixe, zippered plastic bag because they're delicious to eat while frozen on a hot, summer day. Yum.

Peanut Butter Cookies

½ cup butter or shortening
1/3 cup peanut butter
½ cup brown sugar, packed
½ cup granulated sugar
1 egg
1½ cups flour
1 teaspoon baking soda
½ teaspoon salt
½ teaspoon vanilla

Preheat oven to 350°.

Cream butter, peanut butter and sugars together in mixing bowl. Add egg and beat well. Add flour, soda and salt to creamed mixture; mix well. Stir in vanilla. Form dough into 1-inch balls. Place on a baking sheet and press each ball flat with the prongs of a fork or a potato masher. Bake for 12 minutes. Remove from oven and let set up for a minute before removing cookies from pan and placing on a rack to cool.

Praline Cookies

½ cup butter
1 cup packed light brown sugar
½ cup granulated sugar
1 egg
1 teaspoon vanilla
1 2/3 cups flour
½ teaspoon salt
1½ teaspoons baking powder
Pecan pieces

In a mixing bowl, cream butter. Add sugars gradually, creaming well. Mix in egg and vanilla. Add flour, salt, and baking powder; mix well. Drop by rounded teaspoonfuls onto ungreased baking sheets.

Bake 10-12 minutes. Remove from oven; cool cookies on a wire rack.

Place a few pecan pieces on top of each cookie and drizzle cookies with Praline Frosting to keep pecans in place.

Praline Frosting

1 cup packed light brown sugar
½ cup evaporated milk
1 cup powdered sugar, sifted

In a small saucepan, bring brown sugar and evaporated milk to a full boil, stirring constantly. Boil 2 minutes; remove from heat. Blend in powdered sugar; beat until smooth.

Hawaiian Candy

2 cups granulated sugar
1 cup brown sugar
1 teaspoon ground ginger
1 cup crushed pineapple, drained
½ cup cream
2 tablespoons butter
2 teaspoons vanilla
1 cup pecans, chopped

Butter 2 dinner plates or small pans; set aside.

In heavy saucepan, cook sugars, ginger, pineapple and cream over low heat until sugars dissolve; boil to softball stage. Remove from heat and cool to lukewarm. Add butter and vanilla; beat until creamy; stir in nuts. Pour into buttered plates. Let cool and cut into squares.

Microwave Peanut Brittle

½ cup light corn syrup
1 cup sugar
1/8 teaspoon salt
1 cup raw peanuts
1 tablespoon butter
1 teaspoon vanilla
1 tablespoon baking soda
(Butter for foil)

Butter a large piece of aluminum foil and set aside.

Mix syrup, sugar, salt, and peanuts in a 2-quart uncovered casserole dish. Cook 4 minutes on high; stir mixture. Cook 4 minutes more on high; stir in tablespoon of butter and vanilla. Cook 2 more minutes on high; remove dish from oven. Add soda; stir gently. Pour mixture onto buttered foil. Let candy cool and break into pieces. Store cooled candy in a covered container.

Fantasy Chocolate Fudge

3 cups granulated sugar
¾ cup butter
2/3 cup (5-ounce can) evaporated milk
1 (12 oz.) pkg. semi-sweet chocolate chips
1 (7 oz.) jar marshmallow crème
1 teaspoon vanilla
1 c. chopped nuts (optional)

Butter a 13x9-inch pan; set aside.

Combine sugar, butter, and milk in a heavy 3-quart saucepan; bring to a full rolling boil, stirring constantly. Continue stirring over medium heat for 5 minutes to prevent scorching. Remove from heat, add chocolate chips; stir until chips are melted. Add marshmallow creme and vanilla; beat until well blended. Stir in nuts, if desired. Pour into prepared pan and spread evenly. Cool at room temperature.

To serve, cut into 1-inch squares.

Makes approximately 3 pounds.

Variation: Fantasy Red Fudge

Follow directions above, but substitute red semi-sweet chocolate chips and add 3 tablespoons cocoa. Great for Christmas, Valentine's Day, and patriotic holidays.

Chocolate Bon Bons

1 stick butter
1 package shredded coconut
2 boxes powdered sugar
1 can sweetened condensed milk
2 teaspoons vanilla
2 cups pecans, chopped fine
1 stick paraffin
2 packages chocolate chips (18 ounces total)

Mix butter, coconut, sugar, milk, vanilla and pecans in large mixing bowl; roll into 1-inch balls; place on waxed paper. Melt paraffin and chocolate chips in top of double boiler. Dip chocolate balls in hot chocolate mixture; transfer to waxed paper to cool. Store candy in a covered container.

Peanut Butter Fudge

2 cups granulated sugar
2/3 cup evaporated milk
½ cup creamy peanut butter
Dash salt
½ cup butter
1 teaspoon vanilla
Pecans or Walnuts, if desired

Butter 2 dinner plates with additional butter; set aside.

Combine sugar, evaporated milk, peanut butter, salt, and ½ cup butter in heavy saucepan. Mix with spoon; cook, stirring occasionally, until softball stage when a few drops of mixture dropped into a small cup of very cold water forms a soft ball which flattens when removed from the water, or 234°. Remove from heat; add vanilla but do not stir. Let cool to almost lukewarm; beat vigorously with a large spoon until mixture thickens and loses its gloss; quickly stir in nuts. Pour candy into buttered plates. Let cool and cut into squares.

Strawberry Treats

1 can sweetened condensed milk
1 cup coconut, shredded
1 cup nuts, chopped
1 large package strawberry gelatin
Red granulated sugar
Green food coloring
Green granulated sugar
Almond slivers

Mix milk, coconut, nuts and gelatin together in small mixing bowl. Shape mixture into strawberry-shaped balls; roll in red sugar and place on waxed paper. For stems, dip one end of almond sliver in green food coloring and in green sugar; insert one sliver into each strawberry ball. Store candy in a covered container. (Keeps in refrigerator for weeks and may be frozen.)

Chocolate Easter Eggs

Milk Chocolate
Marshmallow Crème

Butter egg inserts of Tupperware egg trays. Melt chocolate in top of double boiler or in microwave. Pour melted chocolate into inserts, enough to coat. Place in refrigerator and let chocolate chill. When chocolate has hardened, remove it from inserts and fill with marshmallow crème; place two egg halves together.

Praline Grahams

1 cup butter or margarine
1 cup light brown sugar
Dash of salt
1 cup pecans
24 graham crackers

Preheat oven to 350°. Place graham crackers in a single layer in a large cake pan or cookie sheet; set aside.

Combine butter, sugar and salt in small saucepan; bring to boil and boil 2 minutes. Remove from heat. Stir in pecans. Pour hot mixture over graham crackers. Bake 10 minutes. Let cool and break apart.

And for my most-requested recipe of all time – PRALINES

*These candies are a creamy version – not the hard and sugary type. Stored in covered tins, with layers separated by waxed paper, they keep well for a couple of weeks. Besides making batches for family and friends, my pralines are sold to caterers in other states who make specialty baskets to sell to banks and business owners and have been private-labeled and sold through bakeries of a supermarket chain. I am now sharing this recipe with **you**!*

Pralines

2 teaspoons baking soda
2 cups buttermilk
1 pound Land O'Lakes® butter
6 cups granulated sugar
2 tablespoons Karo® white syrup
2 teaspoons vanilla
6 cups pecan halves

Have counter space ready – covered with newspaper and waxed paper on top of newspaper.

In a 4-cup pitcher, stir baking soda into buttermilk; set aside.

In an extra-large and heavy-duty stockpot, butter bottom and inner sides all the way to the top; add remainder of butter to pan. Add buttermilk mixture, sugar, and syrup to pan; do not mix. Cook over medium heat, stirring only after mixture melts enough. Leave mixture alone until it reaches softball stage of 234°-238°. (Use cold water test, too. See Personal Cooking Tips for directions.)

Remove from heat and add vanilla. Beat until thickened and candy loses its gloss. Stir in pecans. Using two tablespoons, quickly scoop candies onto waxed paper. Let cool.

Store in covered tins.

Note: I suggest you cut this recipe in half and make it in a heavy Dutch oven. Mixture boils up high at first, so you'll need a larger pan than you think for the amount of ingredients. The first time you make this recipe, it would be wise to have another pair of hands in the kitchen with two more tablespoons to help you scoop out candies before mixture hardens.

Personal Cooking Tips

Foods cooked in a slow cooker, or Crock-Pot®, may be stirred during cooking, but remember that you lose about 30 minutes of cooking time when you lift the lid. Although the aroma may tempt you, resist the urge to peek.

Butter and margarine are interchangeable in *most* popular recipes. Each one-pound package contains four sticks; each stick is equal to one-half (½) cup. Blue Bonnet® regular margarine and Land O' Lakes® lightly-salted butter are preferences of the author.

Vegetable shortening, salad oil, and olive oil may *sometimes* be substituted for one another, but not always. There are exceptions, but a good "rule of thumb" is shortening for baked goods, a good quality salad oil or olive oil for most salads, and any of the three when sautéing. Preferred by the author are Crisco® for shortening and Wesson® or Crisco® for salad oils.

When recipes call for cream of mushroom soup, others may be substituted. Cream of celery soup and cream of potato soup are used most often.

Use dry measuring cups for dry ingredients and liquid measuring cups for liquids. Dry ingredients are spooned into cups and always leveled off, never packed, except for brown sugar.

Any recipe in this cookbook referring to brown sugar means the amount called for is the measurement *after* it is densely-packed with a spoon into a measuring cup – not just pressed into the cup by hand. C&H Pure Cane Sugar® is preferred by the author for all types of sugars mentioned in this personal collection of recipes.

All recipes for milk in this cookbook refer to Vitamin D whole milk unless otherwise noted. Evaporated milk is canned and Milnot® is preferred by the author. Sweetened condensed milk is sweetened, cooked, and canned; Eagle Brand® is preferred by the author.

Cooking and baking times (and temperatures) vary depending on humidity, the size of pots and pans, and the performance of individual ovens; adjust as needed.

To toast walnuts: Spread nuts in a single layer on a baking sheet or shallow pan. Bake, stirring twice, in a 350° oven 10-12 minutes. Remove from oven and let cool.

When making meatloaf or meatballs, form a bite-sized patty and fry it to taste-test before you shape and cook the mixture. Mom tasted a pinch of it raw, but I can't do that.

Store basil with its stems in a vase or jar of water. Keep it on your counter like fresh flowers from your garden. To keep a large quantity of basil fresh for a while, top basil leaves with an opened plastic bag to make a mini-greenhouse.

Home cooks and professional chefs keep measuring spoons attached to the ring, as purchased. I remove and discard those rings. I find it cumbersome to measure in one spoon with the others in the way, and why would I want to wash all of them if I don't use that many each time? If you bake a lot, invest in several sets of measuring spoons and cups.

When making candy that involves beating hot syrup into egg whites, don't try to do it all at once. Check out the recipe in this book for Divinity and see if the directions are an improvement over yours. My mother came up with this method.

If you find it difficult to reach and/or lift down heavy items from upper cabinets, keep smaller amounts of staples handy. I keep shortening in a covered pottery canister that holds about one-third of the big shortening can. To keep bacon grease on hand for frying or for flavoring beans, I store it in a stoneware sugar bowl with lid. The canister and sugar bowl sit beside my stove and make my life easier. If my air conditioner quits, or I'm not cooking often, I store the bacon grease in the refrigerator.

What if you don't have a cooling rack? I didn't have one for years. Spread several layers of newspaper, or paper towels, on top of your cabinet and cover with parchment or waxed paper. This works great for cooling cookies and pralines. Use buttered plates to cool fudge and other candies.

When cooking ribs inside, or out on the grill, soaking them in salt water for a couple of hours will help to tenderize them and make them release from the bone easier.

If you're having difficulty knowing how much salt and pepper you're adding when cooking, try sprinkling in the black pepper before the salt. It makes it easier to see the salt. Or, mix six parts salt to one part black pepper in a large shaker and use that.

I use yellow and white onions interchangeably. If a recipe calls for a sweet onion, white is considered sweeter than yellow. If the dish really needs a sweet onion, choose a Vidalia from Georgia.

As an occasional time-saver, buy vegetables in produce or deli that are already chopped or visit the store's salad bar. Choose fresh vegetables and/or fruits; add your own dressings and special ingredients when you get home for your salad or dip – especially helpful if you only need a small amount of an item or you forgot you were supposed to have a potluck dish ready in a few minutes.

Wear an apron in the kitchen, especially when frying foods. When an injury prevented me from reaching behind my back to tie my apron, I switched to a cobbler's apron that snaps in the front.

How many times have you struggled to seal plastic storage containers? You bought the bowl and lid together; they should seal. Right? Friends say they've discarded dozens of bowls and lunch containers because of the same problem. I fought that battle, even with name brand products, until I stumbled upon a solution. After you put food in the plastic container, hold the lid under hot running water for three or four seconds; shake the lid dry, and seal the container. No problem.

I have two major rules when I'm cooking or teaching someone else to cook, whether in my kitchen or theirs; Impeccably-clean hands and no flying hair. Tie up your flying hair, whether long or short. Wash your hands often – not just a simple rinse under cold water but a real hand wash with hot, soapy water. For some meals, you may wash your hands twenty times so, for convenience, make a half-sink full of hot, soapy water or fill a big mixing bowl of it in your kitchen sink.

Shop the picnic aisle in your favorite grocery or dollar store and pick up a package of plastic bottles for ketchup and mustard. Fill a bottle with your liquid kitchen detergent to keep beside your sink to wash your hands often or put a pan to soak before adding it to your dishwasher.

I keep a package of cheap, food service gloves under my kitchen sink to use when I'm greasing a pan for baking, handling bacon or other meats, preparing vegetables that stain my hands, and other jobs. For more substantial uses, like mixing meatloaf, butchering meat, etc., I use medical gloves. You don't have to, and I didn't for years, but I find it a real time-saver these days.

When mixing cake batter and the recipe says to alternate dry and wet ingredients, always start and end with dry ingredients.

For pies, when fresh fruit seems too juicy, mix 2 tablespoons of all-purpose flour to the sugar called for in the recipe to thicken the pie filling.

For an easy and less messy way to measure shortening, use a glass measuring cup and cold water. Example: You need to measure 2/3 cup shortening. Fill measuring cup with cold water to the 1/3 cup line. Using a plastic spatula, spoon shortening into cup until the water level reaches the 1 cup line. For you to get an accurate measurement, press down on the shortening with the spatula so the shortening is under water. Pour off water and dump spatula into your mixing bowl. This also works for peanut butter.

Chop or shred lettuce with a large, serrated plastic knife to avoid browning. The knife works on citrus, too. What if you don't: have a plastic kitchen knife? .Disposable, serrated knives from fast-food chains will work.

Candy recipes that refer to soft-ball stage sometimes have differing number degrees – any amount from 234°-240° Fahrenheit. I always rely on the old-fashioned test for soft-ball even when using a candy thermometer. Drizzle a few drops of hot candy syrup into a small cup of cold water to see if it forms a ball. Remove the ball and roll it between your fingers. It should be flexible enough to flatten. If the ball does not hold together when you remove it from the cold water, it needs to cook longer. Retest, as needed, until you get the flexible ball for fudge and praline recipes.

If you run short of the sweet chocolate for a recipe, substitute ½ tablespoon granulated sugar and 1 ounce bittersweet, or semi-sweet chocolate, for each ounce of sweet chocolate.

Use a pizza cutter to slice through pastry or noodle dough. Also works well to cut bar cookies, brownies, and thin sheet cakes.

Make a commitment to try a new recipe when you can. Once a week, once a month, or whatever timeframe works for you, experiment. This adds dishes to your recipe box, sometimes challenges you to learn new skills, and lets your creative spirit shine.

Use fresh and local foods as often as you can. Their quality allows your cooking and baking to reach the status of excellence.

Store brands have improved over the years, so do your homework to see if they match the performance of the name brands you normally buy. Your kitchen is the best testing lab around.

Always purchase the best quality foods you can afford, but never let money keep you from cooking for family, even if you're a family of one. Eat right and eat good.

Place a sheet of good-quality plastic wrap directly on the surface of guacamole when you chill it in the refrigerator. This will prevent the dip from discoloring.

Sometimes you have to buy avocados that are not yet ripe. Leave them on your kitchen counter in a brown paper bag for a couple of days. They should be ready to use by then.

Having difficulty getting canned beans, hominy, etc. out of the can? Instead of reaching inside the can with a spoon, try shaking the can prior to opening. Then turn the can upside down and let a can opener slice off the bottom of the can. Vegetables slide right out.

Remember to rinse out cans, jars, and bottles – glass and plastic; put in recycle bin. Choose a large paper grocery sack with handles to set beside your kitchen trash or your lounge chair. Drop newspapers and junk mail into the sack for recycling.

Decorate foods with edible flower blooms like pansies, roses, nasturtiums, and tulips. Rinse well before using. Mix blooms with basil and parsley leaves. Avoid snapdragons and daffodils, no matter how pretty they are.

When deep-frying food in batches, drain on a paper towel-lined platter to remove excess grease or oil. To keep first batches warm while deep-frying later batches, tent food with foil and keep in an oven set at a low 200°.

Sometimes I buy graham cracker crumbs, but what happens when I'm out of crumbs? If I have graham crackers and the recipe calls for crumbs from X amount of crackers, is that before or after the crackers are broken? Is it after the first or second perforated break? Now, I know. One-half cup of finely-crushed graham crackers comes from 7 squares. From which break? I'll let you test.

Kitchen Hints

Never leave potato salad unrefrigerated for more than 2 hours and no more than 1 hour if the temperature is above 90°. *Cook's Country* says potatoes are to blame instead of mayonnaise. Soil and dust harbors the responsible bacteria which thrives on starchy foods like potatoes.

To remove seeds from a cucumber, cut it in half lengthwise and scoop out the seeds with a rounded measuring spoon or a melon baller.

Buy yellow and green bananas. Bright yellow ones, even with a few brown flecks, are ripe and ready to eat. The green ones will ripen, so you'll have fresh bananas all week. Put green bananas in a paper bag if you need them to ripen sooner.

To measure bread crumbs, pack fresh, or soft, crumbs lightly into a measuring cup. Press lightly until level with top of cup. For dry crumbs, spoon into a measuring cup and level it off with a spatula. Do not pack or shake the cup.

For a smooth frosting on your cake every time, apply a crumb coat to cake layers.

To keep cake layers moist, make simple syrup: Bring 1 cup water and 1 cup granulated sugar to a boil; remove from heat; let cool. Apply syrup to top of cake layers with a pastry brush. Depending on frosting choices, you may not want to use simple syrup on the top layer of the cake.

If using fondant, brush corn syrup where fondant meets the bottom of the cake to seal it to the cake plate. Knead in powdered sugar if fondant sticks. Knead in shortening if fondant dries out.

To remove a metallic taste from baby corn, cook 2 minutes in boiling water; drain.

No manicotti noodles? Substitute lasagna noodles which are easier to roll up with filling than stuffing manicotti.

Got milk? Evaporated milk plus water in equal amounts will substitute for sweet milk.

Need sour milk for a recipe? Mix 1 tablespoon vinegar or 1 tablespoon lemon juice to sweet milk to make 1 cup.

Out of honey? Use 1¼ cups sugar plus ¼ cup water.

When cutting onions, do so while holding them under cold running water or place them in the freezer for a short time. Leftover onion should be refrigerated and won't cause tears when you slice or chop it later.

Fresh lemon juice will remove onion scent from your hands. Discarded lemon peelings freshen garbage disposals.

To whip eggs for meringue, bring eggs to room temperature first. This results in greater volume.

When making candy or anything that starts with boiling sugar and water for syrup, keep a bowl of ice water nearby. Even a drop of syrup can pop out and land on your hand. If it does, plunge your hand into the ice water to lessen pain and reduce permanent injury.

Soft-ball stage for candies is 234°-240°, the lower side of the range for fudge, penuche, and cream candies while the high side of the range is for fondant-style candies. Medium ball is 238°-240° for marshmallows. Firm ball is 246°-252° for caramel. Hard ball is 265°-270° for taffy. Crack is 290°-300° for butterscotch. Hard crack is 300°-310° for brittle. (This is pretty much the standard, but information in individual cookbooks does vary. I have one book that disagrees with itself – different numbers on the same page.)

When making layer cakes, fill each pan according to eye. If you have trouble getting the batter evenly distributed, you could purchase a kitchen scale and weigh each pan.

To grease and flour pans: Cover your fingers with plastic wrap, or wear a disposable food service glove, to grease the pans. To make dusting pans easier, use an extra salt shaker filled with flour.

Empty bread bags and ties can be used to store homemade bread loaves and rolls. Great for giving a loaf of bread to a shut-in.

Every savory dish should have at least a pinch of sugar. Every sweet dish should have at least a pinch of salt.

Meat carving is complicated by a dull knife.

Chilled cheese grates easier than room temperature.

Warm serving plates to keep entrees warm. Chill serving plates to keep salads crisp.

Grease muffin tins for individual servings of hot rolls, meatloaf, stuffed green peppers, etc. (Muffin tins keep the peppers standing up straight.) Kids love it when you serve food made just for them; so do adults.

When measuring just a spoon or two of shortening, hold the spoon under hot running water before you measure. Shortening will slide off the spoon into your mixing bowl or skillet. (See the previous tip section for measuring larger amounts.)

Use drinking straws as a tool for pies and cakes. For pies, cut straws in short lengths and insert into slits in the top crust to keep juice from running over the crust and making a mess in the oven. For tall layer cakes, press straws in from the top to keep layers from scooting. Insert wooden skewers into the straws for even more support. If going through cardboard on bottom of layers, like with wedding cakes, forget straws; hammer skewers into the cake. Cut away excess skewers with strong scissors at top of cake.

Plumbers say running ice cubes through your disposal once a week avoids problems.

Surveys show kitchen sponges are germ magnets. Invest in a few dishcloths. Fill a sink with soapy water as hot as you can work with and wash your dishes, if you don't have a dishwasher. Or, wash those dishes and pans you can't put in your dishwasher. Wash down your stovetop and all of your countertops with the dishcloth every day. Change it for a clean cloth daily, and wash with your kitchen and bath towels in hot, soapy water when you do laundry.

Measurements we need often. Do you have them committed to memory?

3 teaspoons = 1 tablespoon
4 tablespoons = ¼ cup
5 1/3 tablespoons = 1/3 cup
8 tablespoons = ½ cup
16 tablespoons = 1 cup
2 cups = 1 pint
4 cups = 1 quart
4 quarts = 1 gallon

How about can sizes? I seldom see a Picnic, 300, or a 1 Tall, but it's important to know.

Picnic – yields 1¼ cups (product)
No. 300 – yields 1¾ cups
No. 1 Tall – yields 2 cups
NO. 303 – yields 2 cups
No. 2 – yields 2½ cups
No. 2½ - yields 3½ cups
No. 3 – yields 4 cups
No. 5 – yields 7 1/3 cups
No. 10 – yields 13 cups

Wash dishes and clean your kitchen after each meal so, when it snows, you can run outside with the kids and build a snowman. Come inside to warm up, drink hot chocolate, and sit by a cozy fire. Read them a story or write one of your own.

Happy cooking to you!

Credits

Recipes:

Thanks to home economics teachers, Nell Fine and Frances Wysowski, and my mother, Dora May Scott, for the first recipes I ever tried to make and to my family, friends, and co-workers who have eagerly taste-tested my recipes throughout the years. I cherish fabulous friends and family who traded recipes with me plus the many publishers of cookbooks and magazines who printed the recipes I shared with them.

Twelve of my favorite recipes were published in More Than We Can Say Grace Over: State Cops Cooking in the Heartland by Oklahoma State Law Enforcement agencies. I assisted with that project, typing, indexing, and bookkeeping – net proceeds of more than $31,000.00 went to Governor Keating's Victim & Family Relief Fund in response to the OKC bombing.

Over time, my recipes have been donated to and published in multiple charity and community cookbooks, newspapers, and magazines, including *Taste of Home,* and their family of cookbooks. I was a Field Editor for Taste of Home for many years.

Original Prose by Barbara Shepherd:

"Forever Young" and "Need More Time?" – Articles published as "Forever young – Edmond grandmother celebrates 13th birthday" and "Need more time? What if you had it?" with 3 photos in *Edmond Life & Leisure*, February 2004.

"Chimes" and "I Remember" – Published in Voices In Time by Shade Tree Creations, 2004.

"Don't Get Caught on the Bridge" – Published in A Centennial Celebration of Oklahoma Stories, 2007.

"Once a Cowgirl" – Published as "The Cowgirl Gazetteer" in Imagination Turned Loose, 2013.

"Taffy Pull" and "Posing for a Photograph" – Published in Beads On a String – Peace, Joy, and Love, 2015.

"Jennifer Eve's New Syndicated Series Focuses on Family" – Article published in *Edmond Outlook*, November, 2005.

Original Poetry by Barbara Shepherd:

"China Painters" –; Poem published in *miller's pond*, Vol.7, Issue 1 and by *H&H Press online poetry magazine* in 2004 due to a second place win in Loella Cady Lamphier Prize for Poetry in 2003; published in Poetry is for Everyone, 2009; published in The Poetry Society of Oklahoma 70th Anniversary Anthology – Candle Flames 1934-2004, 2005.

"Women's Words" – Poem published in *miller's pond*, Vol.7, Issue 1 and by *H&H Press online poetry magazine* in 2004 due to a third place win in Loella Cady Lamphier Prize for Poetry; was a Semi-Finalist in Dallas Poets Annual Competition in 2003; published in A Centennial Celebration of Oklahoma Stories, 2007.

"The Shadow of Fear" and "Life's Thread" – Published in May 2004 edition of Poetry of Today – Christian Poetry (online).

"Stress" and "Turquoise" and "The Necklace" (aka "Conch") and "White Silk" (as prose) – Published in Voices In Time by Shade Tree Creations, 2004.

"Election Day is Coming" – Published in *The Norman Transcript*; Signed/Framed poem donated and sold in a Political Party's Silent Auction at a Presidential Election Watch Party, 2004.

"Scars" and "Almost Well" published in Patchwork Skin, 2005.

"Modern-Day Horse Trader" – Published in A Centennial Celebration of Oklahoma Stories, 2007; published in Poetry is for Everyone, 2009.

"Freedom" and "Creative Spirit" – Published in Poetry is for Everyone, 2009. "Creative Spirit" also in *Lone Stars Magazine.*

"Bare Feet" – Published in travelin' music – A Poetic Tribute to Woody Guthrie, 2010.

"Dusty Bowls" – Published in Elegant Rage – A Poetic Tribute to Woody Guthrie, 2012.

"The Auction" and "Wash Monday" and "Pioneer Stone Masons" – Published in Imagination Turned Loose, 2013.

"Butterfly Garden" – Published in Beads On a String – Peace, Joy, and Love, 2015.

Other awards and publications for prose and poetry not listed.

Index

This book belongs to

_____

My new favorite recipes are:

Page	Title of Recipe

I found more favorites I want to make again:

Page	Title of Recipe

Notes

Notes

ORDER FORM

For additional copies of this book, please order by mail.
Do you want the books signed? _____ *(yes or no)*
(*Note*: E-book will be available later.)

Art Affair
Attn: Cookbook
P.O. Box 54302
Oklahoma City, OK 73154

☐ I borrowed this book from a friend and would like my own copy.

☐ I borrowed this book from a library and would like my own copy.
   Name and Town of Library

_____

☐ I have enclosed a check or money order - payable to Art Affair for $_____ (Cookbooks @ $19.99 each, plus $5.00 shipping/handling per book.)

☐ Please mail _____ copies of Vittles & Vignettes to me.
Please print:
Name

_____

Address

_____

City, State, Zip

_____

ORDER FORM - GIFTS

For additional copies of this book, please order by mail.
Do you want the books signed? _____ *(yes or no)*

Art Affair
Attn: Cookbook
P.O. Box 54302
Oklahoma City, OK 73154

☐ I love this book and want additional copies for gifts.

☐ I have enclosed a check or money order payable to:
Art Affair for $_____

Cookbooks are $19.99 each, plus $5.00 shipping/handling per book.

Please print:

My Name

_____

Address

_____

City, State, Zip

_____

☐ Please mail _____ gift books to me at the above address.

(or)

☐ Please mail books directly to my family/friends/co-workers listed on the next page (s):

#1
Gift Name

_____

Address

_____

City, State, Zip

_____

Gift Card should read:

_____

#2
Gift Name

_____

Address

_____

City, State, Zip

_____

Gift Card should read:

_____

#3
Gift Name

_____

Address

_____

City, State, Zip

_____

Gift Card should read:

_____

#4
Gift Name

_____

Address

_____

City, State, Zip

_____

Gift Card should read:

_____

Please write additional gift names and addresses on a plain sheet of paper. We will be happy to sign and mail gift books to you or to your recipients.

This book is also available at some bookstores and on Amazon.

www.barbarashepherd.com

To pay for **Vittles and Vignettes** *by credit card, please complete this form and mail with your order.* <u>*Your credit card statement will show*</u> **Art Affair** <u>*as a charge.*</u>

Circle: MasterCard or VISA   Amount to charge: $_____

Credit Card Number: _____

Expiration Date: _____

Security Code *(from back of card)*: _____

Billing Zip Code: _____

Signature: _____